WAYS TO DISPLAY

A PRACTICAL GUIDE FOR TEACHERS

Derek Greenstreet

Illustrations : Julia Osorno

ROLLESTON
JUNIOR SCHOOL
- - NOV 1985
Hillsborough Road, Glen Parva
Leicester LE2 9PT
Telephone Leicester 782300

Ward Lock Educational

© **Derek Greenstreet 1985**

First published 1985 by
Ward Lock Educational Co. Ltd
47 Marylebone Lane
London W1M 6AX

A member of the Ling Kee Group

HONG KONG · TAIPEI · SINGAPORE · LONDON · NEW YORK

All rights reserved. No part of this publication except pages 60 — 78 may be reproduced, stored in a retrieval system, or transmitted, in any form or by any means, electronic, mechanical, photocopying, recording or otherwise, without the prior permission of Ward Lock Educational Co. Ltd.

Reprinted 1985

British Library Cataloguing in Publication Data

Greenstreet, Derek
    Ways to display.
    1. Displays in education
    2. Education, Elementary — Audio-visual 8

    I. Title
    372.   13'3042   B1043.6

    ISBN 0 7062 4456 7

Designed and illustrated by Julia Osorno.
Typeset by BLA Publishing Ltd/Composing Operations.
Printed in Hong Kong.

This book is dedicated to all children who share the work they have created and to their teachers who take care to make it possible.

Acknowledgements

The author would like to thank the following people for their assistance in the preparation of this book:
The headteacher, staff and pupils of Ditton CI School, Kent; St James CI School, East Malling, Kent; and Sherwood Park CP Junior School, Tunbridge Wells, Kent; and the staff and pupils of Aylesford CP School, Kent.
Robin Mellor for the photographs on pages 2, 4, 19, 26, 27, 30, 35, 38, 46, 51, 52, 53 and 57 (left).
Vincent Oliver for the photographs on the cover and on pages 3, 10, 35, 36, 37, 39, 48, 56, 57 (right) and 58

Contents

The purpose of display

Basic principles

What is the point of display? Isn't it just a waste of time and money? These are the questions that lurk at the back of many teachers' minds. One aim of this book is to try to answer these questions – to show *why* display is important and *how* it can be done well without too much expenditure of time or money.

Displays should aim to:

1   *Make the environment attractive.*
    Displays can add colour, texture, variety and order, to areas which would otherwise be drab.

2   *Communicate ideas and information clearly.*
    By careful planning and selection of materials, 'thematic' or 'special interest' displays should help children to understand more about the subject.

3   *Stimulate interest and questioning.*
    A display can sometimes act as a starting point for a particular area of investigation. Children studying a display are encouraged to ask questions and seek solutions. Displays can also act as a vital link between the end of one programme of work and the start of another.

4   *Show appreciation of children's work.*
    Good display acknowledges the value

of work well done and the satisfaction which is to be derived from thoughtful and deft presentation. By displaying a child's work you are demonstrating your interest and approval. This can improve your relationship with him and also that between the child and his peers.

5   *Respond to the interests of the children* and acknowledge their many and varied contributions to learning. The teacher has a responsibility to children to display, in context and with sensitivity, the objects of interest they bring into school and any related work.

6   *Reflect the general ethos of the school* by showing that pupils are encouraged to take an interest in their immediate environment and gain an awareness of the world beyond school.

A welcoming book corner, with supporting art work, in an infant school.

Importance of variety

Variety is the keynote to good display throughout a school. Aims and objectives will change according to the nature and content of the display. Sometimes a display can be predominantly instructive, showing objects of interest accompanied by explicit labels and questions to catch the children's attention and encourage them to find out more. At other times, the display will be purely thematic, relating to a particular subject area, topic or seasonal event. Other displays may be composed entirely of children's work linked not by theme or subject but simply by its quality of excellence. Such displays often need little or no explanation; they are there simply to be enjoyed and appreciated.

Developing critical awareness

It is worth remembering that children do not often look carefully at displays which we create for their benefit. They have to *learn* to look at things closely and to make critical and constructive judgements about them. Therefore we have to direct them to look at particular aspects of displays, giving them specific guidance about the kind of things to look for. For example, written instructions can be pinned on the display: 'Look at these two shells. Are they the same shape? colour? size?' 'Touch these interesting objects. Do they feel soft or hard? solid or hollow? Can you name them?' 'These are animal skulls. Can you

guess which animal they belong to? Can you identify these parts: the lower jaw bone? the nostrils? etc'.

Sometimes you can take a whole class to look at a display and use it as a teaching aid. At other times it may be better to send a small group of children to look and ask them to report their findings to the remainder of the class. Approaches like these encourage questioning and discussion and can extend the children's interest beyond the content of the display.

Children should be involved in the planning and setting up of displays on a regular basis. They should be expected to make choices and decisions about the selection of items for display, the type of backgrounds to use and how everything should be arranged. Get them to discuss decisions like these seriously, and help them to find the words to explain their choices.

This kind of experience helps children to become more adept at ordering their own judgements and choices. Critical analysis is an essential ingredient of art education and helping with decisions about setting up displays is a useful way for children to practise that analysis. Throughout this book although, for convenience, I refer to 'you' or 'the teacher', I mean 'you and your class' or 'the teacher and the children'.

Well-presented displays in school undoubtedly convey the general attitudes and values of the school. A school without any stimulating and visually exciting display can appear cold and austere.

'To display children's work with care and dignity is to celebrate that work. It allows us an alternative way in which we can communicate that our schools are places of warmth and care, interest and beauty, excitement and fascination, learning and growth... to child, teacher, parent and visitor alike.'

ILEA Teachers' Art Centre

'This angle? Or that? Which looks best?'

Getting started

Tools and materials

One of the most frustrating aspects of display work in schools is not having the right tools and materials or not being able to find them when they are needed. You can overcome this problem by buying a handyman's simple lightweight tool carrier, available from any DIY store. In this you can keep all the tools and materials required for the majority of display techniques. The carrier can be carried from place to place around the school, keeping everything together and reducing the risk of things being dropped or mislaid. Valuable time is saved and work can be more easily organised.

The following lists include the tools and materials which I have found useful in setting up displays in a variety of situations. (Names and addresses of suppliers are provided on page 58.) It is possible to acquire a wide range of materials suitable for display work from a wide variety of sources at little or no cost. (Try printing works for off-cuts of card and paper and paper mills for end rolls of paper; odd lengths of fabric and quantities of display felt can, on occasions, be salvaged from large department stores when they change their window or internal displays.) A search in the Yellow Pages will reveal a variety of local industries you can approach.

The basic kit of display tools and materials.

1 Rotary trimmer	**4** Carrying box	**7** Ram or push pin tool	**10** Card paper shears
2 Eyelet and hole punch	**5** Vinyl tape	**8** Trigger Tacker staple gun	**11** Mapping pins
3 Dress-making pins	**6** Craft knives	**9** Turikan hook stapler	**12** Bambi stapler

TOOLS (in the carrier)

Trigger Tacker staple gun
Suitable for fixing work to display boards and for covering display boards and units with a variety of materials ready to receive work. The tacker gun will staple paper, card, fabrics and a range of other materials which may be required.

Bambi stapler
Suitable for fixing work to mounts. The staples are very small and unobtrusive.

Ram or push pin tool
For fixing work to pinboard display surfaces using ordinary dressmaking pins.

Sharp scissors or paper shears
For trimming work, cutting around shaped work or preparing mounts.

Sharp craft knife
For trimming and squaring unmounted and mounted work.

Safety rule
A steel or steel edged rule for use with a craft knife.

Staple remover
For removing stubborn staples from display boards and preventing broken fingernails!

Small tack hammer
Suitable for fixing display material to harder surfaces using panel pins or tacks.

Pliers or pincers
Useful for removing tacks, panel pins and broken staples.

Eyelet hole punch
A dual-purpose tool for punching holes in paper, card and fabric and fixing eyelets to prevent the edges of the punched holes from tearing.

Turikan stapler
An inexpensive specialist stapler designed for fixing either open or closed hook staples to work which requires hanging.

Turikan hook staples

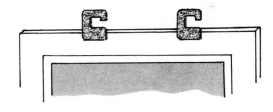

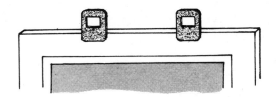

ADDITIONAL TOOLS
(too large for the tool carrier)

Rotary trimmer
Essential for safe trimming of work in preparation for mounting. Produces accurate 'square' corners and edges every time. Safe for children to use when preparing and mounting their own work. Available in a range of sizes.

Large T-square
For marking out large sheets of card and other similar materials.

MATERIALS

Display putty
(e.g. Blu-Tack, Pritt Buddies)
A non-greasy, putty-like substance. Useful for fixing lightweight work to a variety of surfaces without leaving stain marks or causing other damage.

Double-sided transparent vinyl tape
(e.g. Scotch Tape, Sellotape)
Very effective for holding heavier work but tends to mark and damage a number of surfaces.

Mapping pins
(available from most large stationers)
Small, neat pins with round, coloured heads. Unobtrusive when displaying two-dimensional work.

Dressmaking pins
For use with the ram or push pin tool or with thumb pressure into soft pinboard.

Variety of staples
(e.g. Rexel, Vanguard, Ofrex, Bambi)
For use with Trigger Tacker staple gun, Bambi stapler or Turikan hook stapler. Always check size and reference number of staples to avoid damaging stapling machines. It is a good idea to label all staplers with the relevant reference number of staples to be used.

Double-sided adhesive pads
Very effective for holding heavier work but tend to mark and damage surfaces. Remove by damping with a little lighter fluid.

Matt finish transparent vinyl tape
(e.g. Scotch 'Magic' tape, Sellotape, 'Invisible' tape)

A useful adhesive tape as, unlike most normal adhesive tapes, it has a non-reflective surface.

Coloured vinyl tape
(e.g. Sellotape, Scotch tape)
Useful for edging work and making borders. Available in a range of colours including black and white.

ADHESIVES

Adhesives of various kinds are vital for display work. Some, however, need to be used with great discretion and should not be made available to children.

PVA adhesive
(e.g. Berol's Medium, Marvin, Rowney's PVA Medium, Colourblend Medium)
A safe, versatile adhesive. Strong and fairly quick drying when used neat. May be thinned by adding water when less strength is required. Dries transparent and is waterproof in its dry state. May be used as a varnish in its thinned state.

Rubber-based adhesive
(e.g. Copydex, Cowgum, Styccoband, Impact)
Particularly useful for fixing fabric. Peels off most smooth surfaces without marking or damage.

Spirit-based adhesive
(e.g. Evo Stick, UHU, Bostick No. 1 Clear, Superglue)
Extremely strong and ideal for fixing heavy or permanent work. Generally unsafe for children to use because of the chemical make-up of the adhesives.

Glue sticks and pens
(e.g. Pritt stick, Fastik Glue Pen and refills)
Clean and easy to use. A quick and efficient way of mounting two-dimensional work.

Spray adhesive or dry mounting medium
(e.g. Scotch Spray Adhesive)
Particularly useful for mounting photographs and other work carried out on 'gloss' paper. Expensive.

Please note that drawing pins have not been included in the list of suggested fixings. Avoid using drawing pins in display work wherever possible. They are ugly in appearance and their reflective heads divert attention from the work being displayed.

COVERINGS, DRAPES AND PAPERS

Coloured or natural corrugated card
An ideal backing for most displays. It has the advantage of being comparatively cheap. Work can easily be pinned to it. Available in rolls 6ft or 3ft high.

Hessian or paper-backed hessian
A textured fabric ideal for backing display boards and covering display boxes. Available in a range of colours from educational suppliers and decorating shops. Bargain bundles of 'seconds' are sometimes available at greatly reduced prices. (See page 58.)

Display felt
A lightweight felt useful for covering display boards and display boxes. Available in a wide range of colours and shades.

Fabric drapes
Remnants and 'ends of rolls' make attractive background drapes and table covers. Jumble sales are a useful source of these.

Wallpaper
Useful and inexpensive for providing plain, textured or neutral backgrounds. Odd or damaged rolls can be bought cheaply.

Cork tile, carpet tiles
To make attractive display areas on the sides of cupboards and doors or on table tops or other horizontal display surfaces.

Mounting cards and papers
(sugar paper, poster paper, frieze paper, manila card, special effect papers, e.g. brick effect, stone effect, metallic foil, wood grain)
A range of subdued coloured papers and cards should be available for providing attractive backgrounds for displays. Remember, however, that papers fade very quickly in direct sunlight and become easily damaged through constant use. Background papers will therefore require changing regularly.

Mounting two-dimensional work

Two-dimensional work can only be displayed effectively if it is carefully and attractively mounted. Well-mounted work immediately attracts attention and is pleasing to the eye, whereas work which is untrimmed, unmounted or displayed without thought or care shows little respect for the time and effort spent on it.

Backing paper should be heavier in weight than the work to be mounted on it. Creasing and rucking occurs when papers of the wrong weight are used as mounting papers.

The most effective colours to use as mounts are neutral colours or those which are tonally contrasting; black, white, grey, pale blue, cream, fawn, sage, brown, terracotta.

Here are some simple, attractive and yet inexpensive ways of mounting two-dimensional work. All can be achieved without specialist skills and with the minimum of time and effort.

Methods of mounting two-dimensional work

UNMOUNTED WORK
Carefully trimmed but unmounted work.

SINGLE MOUNT
Work should be mounted on a neutral background so as to form a tonal contrast between the mount and the work itself.

LINE AROUND/SINGLE MOUNT
Basically the same as a single mount but made more effective by the addition of a thin line, ideally in black, drawn on the mount around the work.

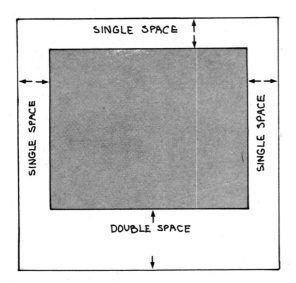

SINGLE SPACE

SINGLE SPACE

SINGLE SPACE

DOUBLE SPACE

PROPORTION OF MOUNT

The proportion of a mount in relation to the size of the work it is to receive is important. As a general guide, the width of the mount appearing beneath a piece of work should be twice the size of that above and to each side of the piece of work.

DOUBLE MOUNT

Double mounting is one of the most effective ways of mounting two-dimensional work. The work should first be mounted on a tonally contrasting background of an appropriate weight, leaving an equal border around the work. The work and mount should then be mounted on a second background paper of a slightly heavier quality, with the larger border below the work as explained above. Light-toned work

should first be mounted on a dark ground followed by a light ground. Dark-toned work should be mounted on a light ground and then a dark ground.

Although double mounting is sometimes considered extravagant, it should be remembered that if you pin through the work and the mounts rather than glueing or stapling the work to them, then the background mounts can be used more than once.

If work is to be glued to a mount, the adhesive should be carefully chosen. Water-based adhesives on cheap papers will often cause them to crease and wrinkle. PVA adhesive, however, is usually satisfactory with most papers and cards, provided that it is applied thinly and spread evenly. Most 'stick' and 'spray' adhesives are reliable, too.

WINDOW MOUNT

This involves cutting card frames, using a sharp craft knife and a safety rule, to the proportions described earlier. The card frame or 'window mount' is then placed over the work to be displayed and pinned into position. Mounts of this kind, particularly if they are cut from good quality card, last well and can be used many times over.

Alternatively, the 'frame' can be attached to a piece of backing card, using either double-sided vinyl tape or a thin bead of PVA adhesive spread around three edges of the backing card, leaving one end open. The work to be displayed can then be slid into the mount between the frame and the backing card. This type of mount is particularly economical and durable and can easily be used again for work of similar size.

FOLDED CARD WINDOW MOUNT

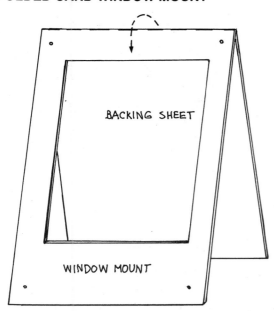

BACKING SHEET

WINDOW MOUNT

An even simpler variation of the window mount is to fold a piece of card in half, having first scored it. Scoring enables thick paper or card to be folded without any trace of creasing or buckling. It is best done by lightly drawing a sharp craft knife, against the edge of a safety ruler, across the surface of the paper or card. The light pressure will be sufficient to break the surface of the paper or card without actually cutting it. The paper or card will then fold neatly and accurately.

After scoring, cut the window in one half of the folded card; the other half will serve as the backing card. The work to be displayed is slotted between the two parts of the mount and pinned into position on a display board.

DURABLE FRAMES

Commercially-produced picture frames are generally very expensive to buy and beyond the budgets of most schools. However, you can often acquire second-hand frames (and some amazing pictures!) at jumble sales and in junk shops. An old frame will be given a new lease of life if you rub it down with sandpaper and apply one or two coats of wood stain or matt finish paint.

Hardboard, or stiff card backing panels, can be cut to fit the frames and held in position by a number of simple 'turn pegs' attached to the back of the frame

Pictures in frames of this kind can be changed quickly and are suitable for a 'changing collection of children's work around a school organised on a subject theme or illustrating a particular technique. Alternatively the frames could hold a changing collection of good quality art reproductions or prints.

A collection of work displayed in this kind of durable frame could be circulated around a group of schools in a neighbourhood so that children in different schools could see each others' work.

Rear of wooden frame showing pegs

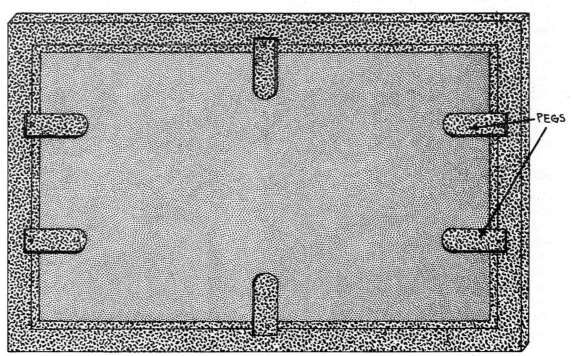

PEGS

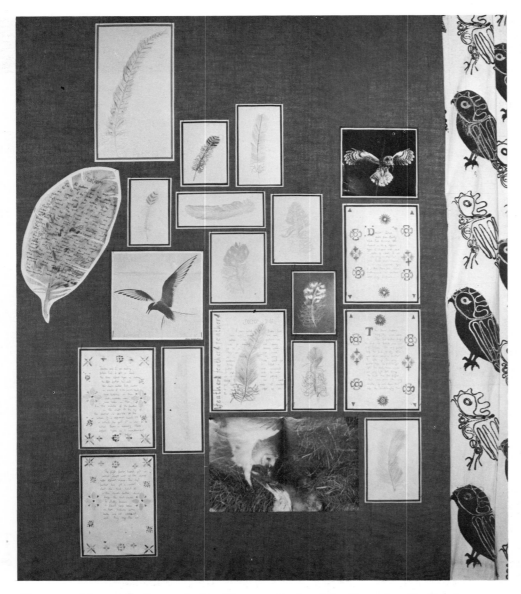

On a corridor wall, decorated written work about feathers is effectively
combined with colour photographs and a drape printed by the children.

'If we put the butterfly here...' Children should play a
full part in creating displays.

Displaying two-dimensional work

Preparing the surface

Once work has been mounted, the next step is to prepare the surface on which it is to be displayed. Various materials can be used, depending on the nature of the display and the effect required.

Hessian fabric or paper-backed hessian in subdued or neutral colours provides a slightly textured background which is particularly attractive.

Display felt offers a much smoother surface and a wider choice of colours.

Corrugated card, either coloured or natural, makes a most effective background material as it has a built-in texture of lines which can be displayed either vertically or horizontally and which automatically act as a guide when lining work up. Work can be pinned to the raised corrugations with dressmaking pins.

Decide whether to use the corrugations vertically or horizontally

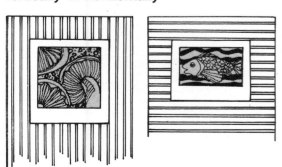

Display papers vary considerably in weight, quality and suitability. The range of colours available is almost limitless but display papers have the disadvantage of fading rapidly and so some people prefer to use white card or paper or natural hessian.

Fixing the backing material to the board

The backing material is best fixed to the display board by using a Trigger Tacker gun which will 'fire' staples through the backing material into most surfaces. An electric version is now available which will penetrate really hard surfaces. An ordinary table stapler, opened out flat, will act as a 'tacker' stapler if the staples are being driven into a reasonably soft surface. Alternatively, a ram or push pin tool will drive dressmaking pins or small tacks into most soft to moderately hard surfaces. Both these fixings are extremely neat and unobtrusive.

When fixing the backing material, it is important to make sure that it is pulled tight so that the display surface is left free from wrinkles or creases. A display board with badly fitting backing material looks ugly and creates problems when you try to attach work to it.

When you have fixed the backing material to the board you can frame the whole board with an edging strip of some kind. Medium weight card of a neutral colour, cut into narrow strips on a rotary trimmer, is ideal for this purpose.

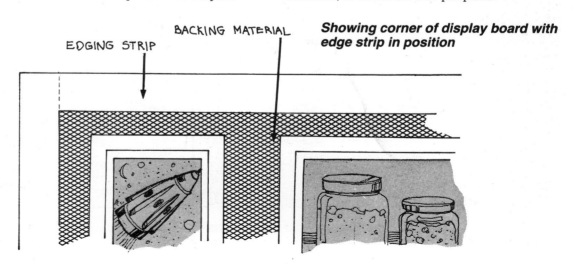

EDGING STRIP

BACKING MATERIAL

Showing corner of display board with edge strip in position

11

Positioning work

For best effects, the work must be well positioned on the display board. There is nothing more unsightly than work which is crooked, too close together, overlapping or generally carelessly displayed.

There are no set rules for the way in which work should be arranged. It is largely a matter of personal preference and a feeling for an arrangement that simply looks right. With experience you develop an eye for a good arrangement. However, the following guidelines may help.

1   Display all work in an orderly manner. Whenever possible aim for a geometric arrangement.

2   Aim for an overall balance between large and small work.

3   It is often best to arrange work on a grid system by using vertical and horizontal guidelines to form links between the various pieces of work being displayed.

4   Display at a level where children can easily see the work. Remember that a child's eye level is very different from an adult's. (Teachers should occasionally put themselves on the same eye level as the children they teach in order to see for themselves just how different the world looks!)

5   Do not be tempted to put too much material in your display. This is a common mistake which almost always lessens the impact and effectiveness of a display.

6   Be selective. Always make sure that you are actually conveying what you intended.

7   Whenever possible display in good light, whether natural or artificial.

8   Displays usually require some explanation. Labels and captions should be carefully prepared and positioned.

9   Consider mounting one key piece of work differently from all the other work in the display to draw particular attention to it.

10   Finally, remember that even rather mediocre work will be greatly enhanced if it is carefully mounted and thoughtfully displayed and that this will provide much encouragement to its originator.

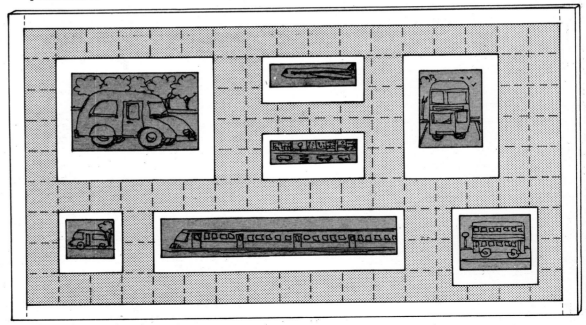

You can mark out a grid with faint chalk lines to help you align work horizontally and vertically.

Marking grid lines

A piece of string rubbed with chalk and stretched across a display board will leave a faint line if pulled out and allowed to snap back onto the surface of the board. This is a quick and useful method of marking out lines for a simple grid. These lines can easily be removed by a light brushing once the display is in position.

Alternatively, a blackboard-size T-square, which can be slid along the vertical and horizontal edges of a display board, will establish accurate grid lines which may be lightly marked. It is particularly helpful to line up and position work in this way in the early days of setting up displays. After some experience of arranging work on display boards it is usually possible to dispense with guidelines or other aids altogether.

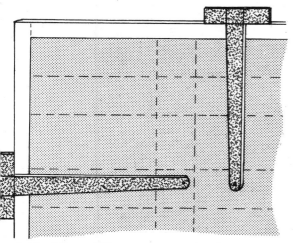

A blackboard T-square can also be used to mark out grid lines.

Including other materials

So far, mention has only been made of children's work. Frequently, however, displays include a variety of materials drawn from many sources including commercially produced materials, photographs, maps, charts as well as children's work.

In displays of this kind you have to establish a balance between the related parts. For example a travel poster might be used as the key item in a wall display of work about a particular country. The poster could be placed centrally or to one side of the display with the related work positioned around it, possibly linked by coloured threads and mapping pins.

A commercially-produced map makes a centrepiece for a display of related work — linked by coloured thread and pins.

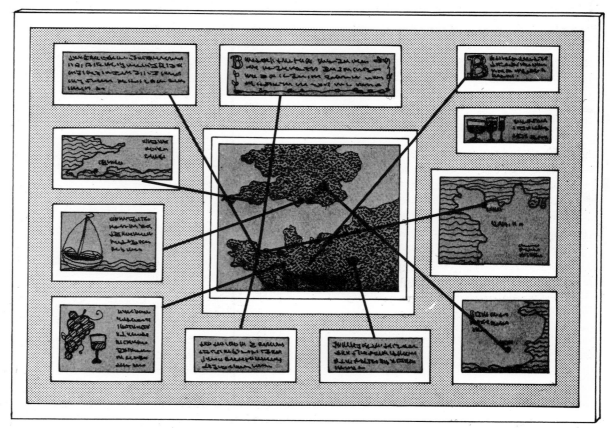

Displaying three-dimensional objects

When displaying three-dimensional objects there are some further considerations. The three main ones are:

1. How much space is available and how much will the display require?
2. Will the display present any safety risks?
3. Are the items being displayed likely to be damaged or broken by people going past the display or by being handled?

In the past, most three-dimensional displays in public places like museums were housed behind glass. This was often done in schools, too, and a few schools still persist with this practice which imposes severe restrictions upon the scope of a display. However, most schools have now adopted a quite different philosophy about three-dimensional displays: the emphasis is on the importance of observing things closely and of handling them when appropriate.

With these points in mind, three-dimensional displays clearly need to be sited very carefully, whether within the classroom or in other strategic positions around the school.

Continual movement past a display may cause problems. Such questions as 'Will the display be stable?' 'Does it protrude too far?' 'Will it obstruct free movement?' must be asked, and satisfactorily answered, before setting up a display.

Involving the children

The question of handling objects on display is particularly important. If children are to be encouraged to touch and feel certain objects, then the intention should be clearly conveyed by appropriate labels, headings and captions. 'Is this rough or smooth?' 'Which will hold most?' 'Which is heavier?' and other similar questions all make the invitation to handle objects on display perfectly clear.

When displaying three-dimensional objects you must consider the display surface, the background and the size and nature of the objects themselves.

Surfaces and containers

You don't have to buy expensive items of furniture or special display units to create eye-catching three-dimensional displays. All sorts of readily obtainable materials can be adapted to make attractive and functional display surfaces; for example, old desks, tables, chairs, tea chests, stage block units, large cardboard cartons, stout cardboard boxes, hoops, tins of various sizes, tin lids, cake bases, baking trays, glass jars, bottles and an almost unlimited number of other items which may normally be considered as useless waste.

Furniture, stage blocks, and cardboard cartons

Old desks and tables can be converted to make robust and attractive display units.

First, the working surface should be covered with a suitable material. If cost permits, glue or tack on a new surface of natural wood or laminate panels in simulated wood, brick, tile or stone. Alternatively, the working surface can be covered with cheaper materials such as hessian, felt, rush matting, cork tiles, carpet tiles, vinyl floor covering or display papers. These materials can be fixed using either a Trigger Tacker gun, double-sided vinyl tape or a strong impact adhesive. The choice depends upon the nature and permanency of the material being used.

Once the surface has been covered, a skirt of corrugated cardboard or fabric can be stapled around the frame of the desk or table with a Trigger Tacker. (Keep the skirting material as taut as possible.)

Old stage block units, which may be too splintered for use in P.E. or drama lessons, make excellent display units. They can be covered in the same way as desks and tables. If stage blocks are not available stout cardboard cartons, used in packing television sets and washing machines, make very good substitutes. Ask for them in appropriate shops. Cover

Cover stage blocks, packing cases or cardboard cartons with cork tiles, carpet tiles and corrugated cardboard to make display stands.

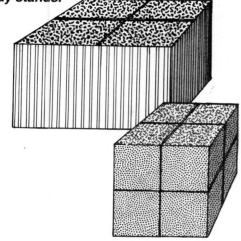

Different-sized packing cases make a multi-level display unit.

the boxes using some of the materials suggested above, but you may find when covering them that staples pull out too easily. If so, then use double-sided tape or pins pushed through with a ram or push pin tool.

A range of different-sized boxes can be sited together to provide a larger, multi-level display area for use in a school entrance hall or a corner of a classroom.

Old chairs, which have either been stripped down to the natural wood and repolished, or painted in attractive, contrasting colours make excellent display stands for ceramic and other craft work. They look particularly effective when used in conjunction with boxes or small wooden tables. The addition of trailing pot plants almost always enhances a display of this kind.

Strip and paint old chairs and use them for display stands.

Interesting display stands

Display stands can be produced by using parts of broken or unwanted school furniture. Parents could perhaps help with this. The original pieces of furniture can be dismantled and then reassembled into unusual shapes and forms. Cut the pieces into the shapes required and assemble them with materials such as hoops, dowel rods and string. Paint the finished product with quick-drying emulsion paint.

Old desk tops, scrap wood and a discarded hoop are reassembled to make a display stand.

Containers for small objects

When small objects like marbles, pebbles, shells, beads etc. are used in a display, there are specific problems. If they are to be handled, they must be accessible; but they are easily lost or knocked off the display. They have to be contained in some way without being concealed. There are some simple solutions to this problem. You can display them in jars and bottles of the type cider and some wines are sold in, or in old tin or box lids, with the rim decorated with coloured vinyl tape and a mat of coloured card or paper inside. The items can be easily retained, handled and returned to the correct area of the display.

Contain small objects safely in tin and box lids.

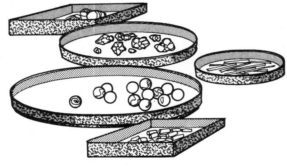

Sand, pebbles, woodshavings or sawdust make an effective display surface — keep them in place with a raised edging strip.

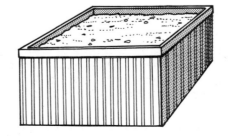

Mats of various kinds are useful to isolate certain items within a display. Cut them from carefully chosen coloured display papers or use inexpensive bought materials such as cork tiles, carpet tiles, rush mats or even certain kinds of door mat.

It is sometimes very effective to use appropriate 'natural' surfaces: for example, shells can be arranged on sand, driftwood on pebbles, fungi on bark or leaves and old wood-working tools on wood shavings or sawdust. If you are doing this, glue or tack a raised edging strip of wood or strong card around the display surface. Alternatively, a tray, made to the exact size of the display box, can be used with it.

Variety of levels

It is important with three-dimensional display to present the work on a variety of levels. In the same way that a mount draws attention to a piece of two-dimensional work, so isolating or raising a piece of three-dimensional display material up above other items on display will attract attention to it. It is important, therefore, to choose key items which will be displayed more prominently than others.

Display platforms

Simple display platforms or stands can be made by covering the sides of tins and small boxes with display paper, patterned self-adhesive vinyl, paper-backed hessian or corrugated cardboard using either an impact adhesive or double-sided vinyl tape.

Cardboard tubes (from the inside of rolls of fabric or paper) can be accurately cut by holding them lightly in a vice and sawing with a fine toothed hacksaw (the type used for balsa wood is ideal) to provide a set of display stands of varying heights ranging from about 5 cm to 15 cm tall. A mat of coloured display paper or card can be cut and fixed to the display surface.

Turn an old tin upside down and cover it with corrugated card, with a mat of display paper on top for a neat display platform.

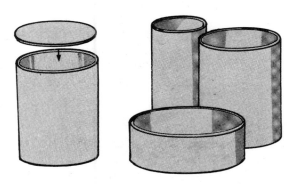

Cardboard tubes, sawn into varying lengths, make more display stands.

MAKING DISPLAY PLATFORMS

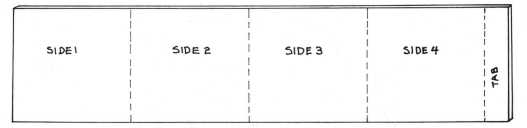

Score and fold strong card as indicated by the dotted lines. Stick tab to back of side one using either PVA glue, double-sided vinyl tape or staples.

TOP FACE

Cut a square of card slightly larger than the base for the top face

Stick the top to the base with a bead of PVA glue round the edge.

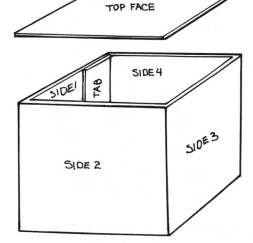

TOP FACE

SIDE 1 TAB SIDE 4
SIDE 2 SIDE 3

**4 sides + tab for square and rectangular forms.
3 sides plus tab for triangular forms.
6 sides plus tab for hexagonal forms.
8 sides plus tab for octagonal forms.**

A variety of shaped display platforms can quickly be made by marking out, cutting, scoring, folding and sticking thick (twelve sheet thickness) mounting card. A bead of PVA adhesive spread around the top edge of the shape will hold the top face in position. To save space when the display platforms are not being used, you can make each platform slightly smaller than the previous one so that they will stack inside each other for storage.

Where coloured card has been scored and folded a white edge of card appears. This can be disguised by colouring it in with a matching felt-tipped pen.

Decorative containers

Not all schools possess attractive vases, flower bowls and storage containers, so card structures like these, but without the addition of a top face, can be used to disguise the jam jars, cut-down plastic bottles and margarine tubs so frequently used in schools for flowers, bulbs, pencils etc. It is important that children become accustomed to seeing well-made artefacts so that their own aesthetic judgements may be sharpened and, wherever possible, schools should buy craft pottery, earthenware containers and stoneware jars for use in displays around the school.

Many potters will sell their 'seconds' cheaply to schools.

Other useful objects

You can introduce a range of man-made and natural objects into displays to provide different levels and effects. Builders' bricks, decorative walling blocks, pieces of slate, lengths of polished wood, various geological stones and polystyrene blocks can all be incorporated into three-dimensional displays.

Disguise a jam-jar with a cardboard tube covered with decorative paper.

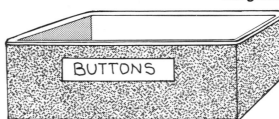

A scored and folded cardboard surround for a margarine tub.

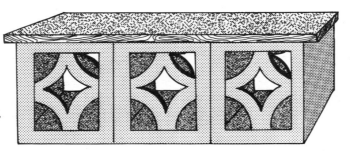

Put concrete wall blocks and a polished wood top together to make a display stand.

Beg a slice of a tree trunk from a saw mill for a fine background for an autumn display.

A dreary doorway in a primary school hall made into a useful display area for two- and three-dimensional work by the addition of corrugated card backing and covered display boxes.

Finding a space

Unfortunately, many schools are poorly equipped with display boards and units and do not always have obvious spaces where these could be fitted. Walls are often broken up by large areas of window glass, P.E. equipment, pipes and other obtrusions which make the displaying of work difficult. Most teachers therefore have to use other areas for display or find ways of adapting existing facilities.

Furniture arrangement

From time to time you should stand back and look at how your classroom is organised to check whether you are making the best, most efficient use of space and facilities. Sometimes rearranging the furniture is all that is ncessary to provide new opportunities for display work in classrooms or other areas of the school. A little time spent in measuring and planning and then a short burst of furniture moving can bring about a completely changed environment. Furniture standing around the outer walls of a classroom restricts the possibilities for display. Simply turning it so that it stands at ninety degrees to the wall creates 'bays' or 'interest areas' and moving it to a central or corner position may reveal other display areas.

Wall space

Classrooms which have large areas of wall space taken up with glass present particular problems. One effective solution is to use large rolls of coloured or natural corrugated cardboard. The cardboard can be unrolled around the corner of a room with a pillar of rolled cardboard at each end to hold it up. In the classrooms where this kind of problem is most likely to arise, the light will not be significantly reduced by cutting out an area of glass in this way. Two-dimensional work can be pinned to the corrugated cardboard and three-dimensional work can be displayed on units in front of it.

If you have work tops around the outer walls of your classroom, you can put narrower rolls of corrugated cardboard on top of them.

Good use of a narrow high level display area in an infant library with pictures of an extract from a favourite book.

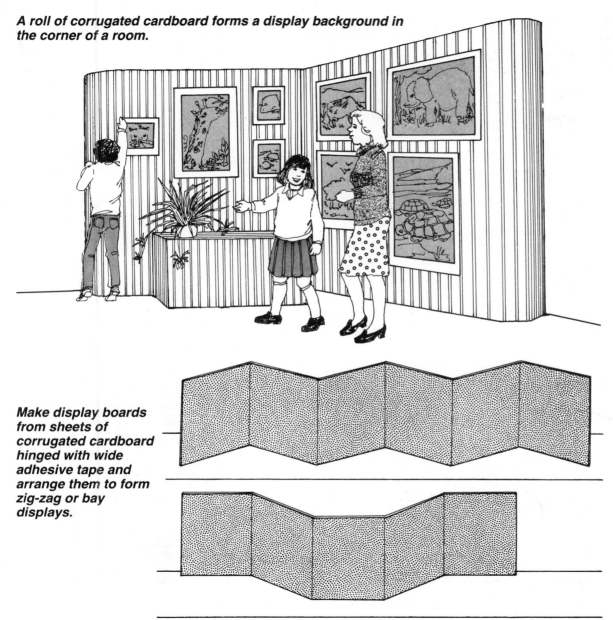

A roll of corrugated cardboard forms a display background in the corner of a room.

Make display boards from sheets of corrugated cardboard hinged with wide adhesive tape and arrange them to form zig-zag or bay displays.

Cheap display boards

Corrugated cardboard packing cases or cartons are excellent for making very cheap yet effective display boards. Look for cartons where the corrugations have been sandwiched between sheet cardboard.

Cross-section of the kind of cardboard to look for.

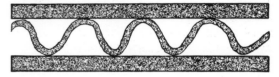

Cut them up carefully using a sharp craft knife and you will have large sheets of thick display board which will easily take pins and even staples. Trim the pieces of board accurately to equal size and then cover them with display paper, hessian or felt which can be pinned or taped onto the back. The separate pieces of board can then be assembled, using wide adhesive tape on the back so as to make a continuous, hinged run of display boards. These joined boards can be used to form zig-zag arrangements, or to make simple bays in which displays can be placed.

Single pieces of this covered cardboard can be used as independent display boards. Covered on one side only they can be hung on the walls; covered on both sides, they can be hung where they can be viewed from both sides and the display space is doubled. If display boards are to be hung in this way, either eyelets or Turikan hook staples should be attached to the corners to prevent the line used for hanging pulling through the display boards. Transparent fishing line, which is very strong but unobtrusive, is most useful for hanging display boards and other items.

Similarly, you can tack appropriately covered display boards to old wooden hoops bound with strips of coloured paper, ribbon (florist's ribbon is ideal) or coloured vinyl tape. These hoops can be suspended to create additional display where space is in short supply.

Tack display boards to old hoops bound with strips of coloured paper or ribbon.

A WINTER DAY

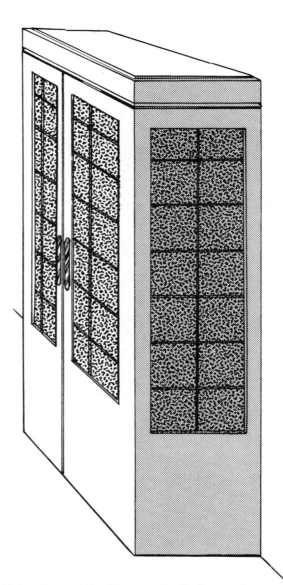

Extend your display area by fixing cork tiles or lightweight pinboard to cupboard doors and sides.

Finding other spaces

The space above the children's heads is an area which is seldom exploited to the full. Although viewing work hung from ceiling height is not ideal, it is a way of displaying large-scale, bold work.

There are other areas which can be adopted as display spaces in most classrooms. Sides and doors of cupboards are particularly suitable. Mounted work can be attached directly using display putty but more permanent display areas are created by fixing lightweight pinboard or cork tiles to available surfaces.

Cork tiles and fibre mat floor tiles will stick directly onto brick or plaster walls if recommended sticking instructions are followed. They make additional and attractive display areas. Mapping pins will fix neatly into both of these surfaces.

Pegboard was fitted in many classrooms at one time but teachers never found it very useful as special pegboard fittings had to be bought to hold items in place. Also, pegboard is extremely hard and will not easily accept staples or pins. If you have pegboard, it is probably worth covering all or some of it with pinboard or cork or mat tiles etc.

Another way of increasing display space is to fix high level back boards to old desks or tables. This is another job that parents can undertake.

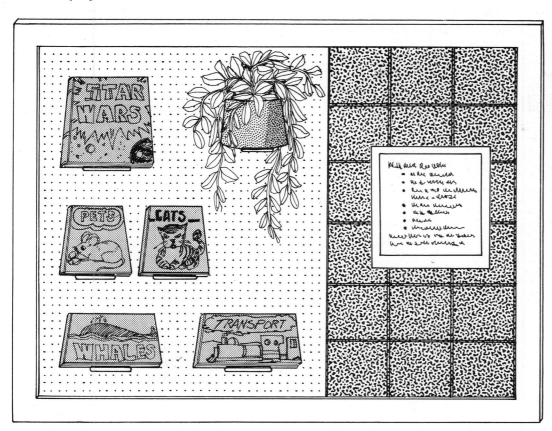

Fibre floor tiles cover half of a pegboard to make display easier.

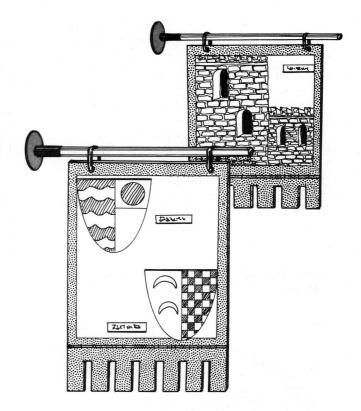

Screw towel rail sockets to suitable wall surfaces and insert dowels to provide 'inn sign' displays.

'Inn sign' displays

Towel rail sockets screwed to any suitable surface make it possible to have 'inn sign' displays. These are hung from pieces of dowelling fitted into the sockets. Turikan hook staples can be used to attach the work to the rods. (Make sure the projecting ends of the dowelling are above child-eye height.) Work on heraldry, advertising, signs and symbols, or any bold, pictorial subjects look particularly well displayed in this way. When the display is over, the rods are taken down but the sockets can be left on the wall for another occasion. This kind of display is particularly effective if situated above a work surface, so that three-dimensional work or book displays can be incorporated.

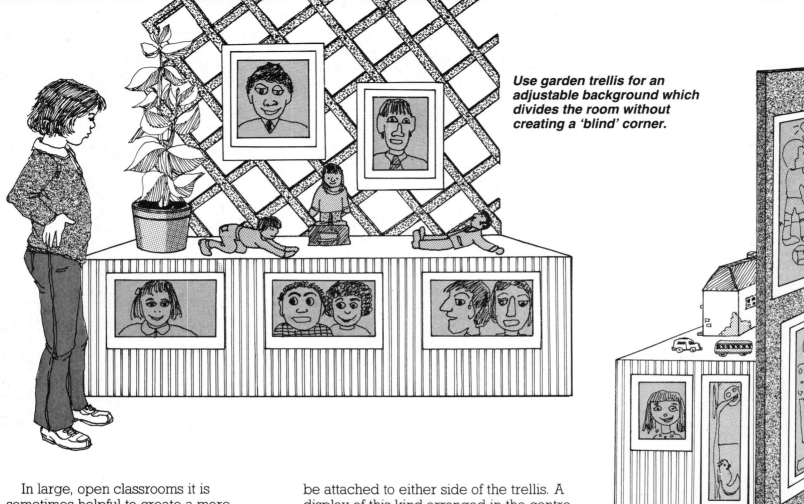

Use garden trellis for an adjustable background which divides the room without creating a 'blind' corner.

In large, open classrooms it is sometimes helpful to create a more homely atmosphere by linking different levels of display. A useful material for this purpose is criss-cross garden trellis which is available in wood or plastic from most DIY shops. Fixed at ceiling height to a beam or batten, the trellis can be extended and fixed at the lower end to a display unit. Two-dimensional work can be attached to either side of the trellis. A display of this kind arranged in the centre of a classroom has the effect of creating a room divider without obstructing the view of any part of the room.

The setting up of displays in corridors and passages is dealt with in the chapter on Book Displays (page 40.)

Give an old desk a corrugated cardboard skirt and a pinboard backing to make a 2D/3D display unit.

Fabrics, drapes and backgrounds

The background to a display is very important. Usually it is best to keep it simple. Displays are often presented against totally unsuitable backgrounds which destroy their impact and effectiveness. As a general rule, bright colours and heavier patterns are to be avoided as work displayed against them tends to be 'lost'.

Choose, if you can, neutral or subdued colours as backgrounds and, whenever possible, provide a textured surface which will contrast with the clear lines of the items being displayed. (See also page 11 for remarks on materials for covering display boards.)

Fabrics and drapes

Including fabrics and drapes in a display adds to the general effect. Fabric is particularly useful for covering large areas of wall which have been made unsightly by pipework, cables and other eyesores. It can also be used instead of corrugated cardboard to form skirts around old tables and desks. Gather it into loose pleats and staple it into place using a Trigger Tacker gun.

By using fabric drapes, links can be made between two- and three-dimensional displays. A length of fabric, attached to one corner of a display board and allowed to freely drape down to a display unit beneath it, leads the eye from one part of a display to another.

Fabric makes an effective link between a two-dimensional and a three-dimensional display.

You can speed up the whole process of building a display by the thoughtful and selective use of fabric. It can hide a multitude of sins beneath it! It is particularly useful in the making of a multi-level surface for displaying three-dimensional work.

Arrange a variety of containers of different shapes and sizes on a table which has been skirted with corrugated cardboard, and drape the fabric over the containers to cover them completely while allowing their shapes to show. This gives you 'platforms' on which items can be displayed.

Pinboard on battens

Where large expanses of wall are broken by light switches and power points, it is not usually possible to fix permanent display boards to the walls. However, this space is too valuable to lose. The problem is to devise ways of using the space while keeping the switches, power points etc. accessible. A satisfactory solution, although it involves some expense, is to fit varnished or painted battens to the wall and attach panels of pinboard to them. These can be arranged in 'random' formation so that switches, power points etc. are left exposed. Narrow shelves can be fitted into some of the 'spaces' and used for the display of small three-dimensional work.

A random arrangement of scrap containers (right) covered with a fabric drape, provide an attractive and quickly assembled multi-level display surface.

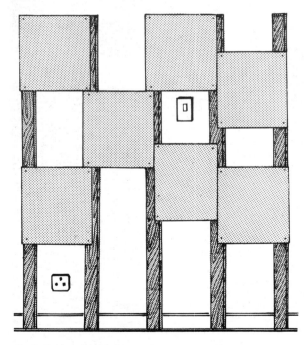

Panels of pinboards, fixed to battens, allow wall space to be used without obscuring plugs and switches.

Using natural materials

The most effective backgrounds of all are often 'natural' materials or materials which have been brought into school to echo the general theme of the display. Brick-faced walls, stone cladding and wood panelling are found in some schools and provide excellent backgrounds for displays. Fishing nets, bead curtains, bamboo screens or even woven mats hung as tapestries can make an enormous contribution to the overall appearance of a display.

It is a valuable exercise for any teacher to go around a school building on the lookout for features which might lend themselves as suitable backgrounds for display.

Using window space to advantage in an infant school interest display.

Labels, captions and headings

Many thoughtful and otherwise attractive displays are spoilt by poorly formed lettering and labelling.

Lettering

Pen lettering is a skilled craft which many teachers consider to be beyond them. However, with the range of materials available today, pen and brush lettering has been greatly simplified and can be mastered providing that sufficient time and effort is given to it. Alternatively, there are many other methods of lettering which are within the scope of any teacher. The following list suggests the breadth of choice available.

Pen lettering, brush lettering

Lettering pens are now available in many forms ranging from the widest chisel-tipped felt pens, which may be either water- or spirit-based, to very refined calligraphers' nibs designed specifically for the most decorative script writing.

then.

Letters formed with an italic style felt-tipped pen.

Spirit-based felt-tipped markers are waterproof and are therefore reasonably permanent. Water-based markers will run or smudge if they come into contact with water. Most felt-tipped markers have either a chisel tip or round tip. A range is now available which enables the writer to produce a well-formed italic hand.

Lettering brushes are also produced in a range of sizes with a variety of shaped tips. You can experiment with these until you find a suitable style. Lettering brushes are best used in conjunction with black or coloured drawing inks.

Stencil letters with the characteristic 'breaks'.

BACK

The same lettering with the breaks filled in.

Stencils

Stencils are available in a wide range of lettering styles. The appearance of some stencilled letters can be rather stiff and unattractive and many of them have the characteristic stencil 'breaks'. With practice, by moving the stencil as you work, it is possible to stencil letters without leaving the breaks. However, it is easier, especially for children, to stencil the letters first and then go back and fill in the breaks. Most round-tipped felt pens work well in stencils without smudging.

Letter templates

I do not favour the use of templates in most areas of school work but they do have a positive role to play in raising the standard of lettering in displays. A number of firms produce a range of wooden or plastic letter templates. These can be drawn around on paper, coloured and then cut out, or they can be drawn around directly on coloured paper or card and then cut out. Like stencils, letter templates give a certain degree of uniformity to headings or captions in an individual display or throughout a whole school.

A group of parents or older children, who are skilled at cutting, can make a stock of letter shapes from templates to be used as they are required. They can be stored in small plastic kitchen containers or snap-sealed polythene bags.

Dry transfer lettering

This is the 'rub down' lettering (e.g. Letraset) available in a variety of styles from most stationers. It is easy to apply and leaves no mess as the letters are simply transferred from a backing sheet onto the display material by applying light pressure with a pencil or similar tool.

This system of lettering gives a very professional finish but it is expensive and consequently out of the question for most schools.

Typewriting

Typewritten labels have the disadvantage of being rather small and therefore difficult to read from a distance. They are mainly suitable for naming work or adding other similar 'credits'. A 'jumbo' typewriter is a great help.

The grid system

You can develop a very good standard of freehand lettering by using a simple grid system to help form the letters. The spacing of letters in captions and headings is critical. Different letters of the alphabet take up varying degrees of space. Discuss this with the children and show them how:
Some letters fit into a square:
A C D G H M O Q T W
other letters fit into half a square:
B E F J I L P S
the remainder fit into approximately three-quarters of a square:
K N R U V X Y Z

Also, a general guide is to aim for regular spacing between letters, based on the distance between the nearest point of contact between them. In the word WEATHER the distance between the top of the W and the top of the E should be equal to the distance between the bottom of the E and the bottom of the A. Similarly, the same distance should be left between the top of the A and the top of the T.

You can vary letters by scaling down the size of the grid, sloping the sides of the grid boxes or rounding the corners of the letters formed (see illustrations).

LETTERING ON A GRID *Use a simple grid system to help form letters.*

Different letters take up different spaces.

Some letters fit into a square.

You can round the letter corners.

Some into half a square.

Some need three-quarters of a square.

You can slope the grid boxes.

Some lower-case letters need two boxes.

Although it is initially time-consuming, it is worth preparing a 'master chart' of all the letters, numbers and other signs and symbols which you regularly need. All future lettering can be either traced or photocopied from the master. The letters can then be decorated, cut out and mounted to form headings and captions for displays.

Still using the grid system it is possible, with a little imagination and experimentation, to vary the shape of letters. Once you have become confident using the grid system you will find that you and the children can devise endless variations.

If you would like a co-ordinated style of lettering for everyday notices and labels throughout the school, you can photocopy the pages at the back of the book.

Forming headings from objects
If you find traditional lettering techniques difficult, other possibilities are worth considering. An effective way of producing eye-catching headings or captions is to match the lettering to the theme of the display. For example, a display about trees could be headed with lettering made by forming the word 'Trees' with twigs cut and stuck onto a card background with PVA adhesive.

MORE LETTERING STYLES

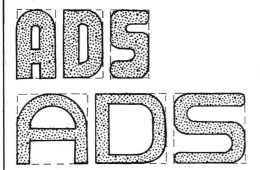

You can use a combination of grid sizes.

Make the letters broader or narrower for further variation.

After some practice with the grid system, the variations are limitless.

Form letters from objects related to the theme of the display.

30

Similarly, a display about birds could be headed with the word 'Bird' spelt out in feathers. A project on holes could have metal or rubber washers to spell out the word.

Once made, these headings can be retained for further use. Over a period of time, a school can build up a stock of headings covering major primary school themes. Here are some suggestions but you and your class will be able to devise many more to suit the work you have been doing. (PVA adhesive, used either neat or thinned, will stick most materials to most surfaces.)

More lettering ideas

Sticking coloured counters to card or pressing drawing pins with coloured heads into card are quick ways to form letters. Lightly pencil in the letter shapes first to ensure that they are uniform size and correctly spaced.

Stick coloured counters to card or press in colour-headed drawing pins for interesting captions.

Textured letters make effective headings. Cut letter shapes from card (using a template if you like) and spread them with a thin film of PVA adhesive. While the adhesive is still wet, the letters can be sprinkled with sand, sawdust, seeds, cork chippings, glitter, aquarium gravel or similar materials. (This approach is really only suitable for lettering made on a fairly large scale.)

Re-useable fabric letters can be made by sticking oddments of fabric onto thin card with fabric adhesive. Cut out the letters and stick small pieces of 'Velcro' to the back of them and they can be attached to display boards covered with felt or similar fabrics.

Headings, captions and labels are an important feature but they should not be so prominent that they detract attention from the items being displayed. Lettering should be clear and easily readable. As a general guide, neutral colours are best as a background. Black on white is the easiest to read.

Labels which stand out

You can fix the heading or label directly on the surface of the display board using unobtrusive dressmaking or mapping pins. However, where the headings or captions in a display are conveying information or instructions you may want to give them greater emphasis. This can be done in a variety of ways. The labels can be raised off the surface of the display board by sticking them onto the sleeve of a matchbox or another small box which is

Topic/theme	Suggested material to form letters
Trees	Twigs
Birds	Feathers
Sea, seaside	Shells or small pebbles
Jokes	Letters cut from comics
Costume, fashion	Buttons or letters cut from fabric scraps
Building	'Lego' bricks or small blocks of wood
Foreign countries	Stamps
Farms	Straw
Wild animals	Cut out letters decorated with patterns depicting the skins of animals — giraffe, tiger, leopard, zebra etc.
Money, shopping	Real, cardboard or plastic coins
Holes	Rubber or metal washers
Romans	'Mosaic' lettering
Food	Cake decorations or pasta

then either pinned or stuck to the display board.

A similar effect can be achieved by writing on card which is then scored and folded to make three-dimensional forms. The finished product can either be stuck on the display like the boxes or can stand beside three-dimensional displays.

Mount labels on matchbox sleeves

Make free-standing labels from scored and folded card.

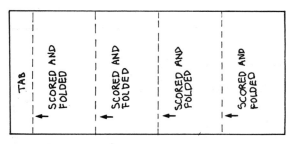

Four folds make a square or rectangular form.

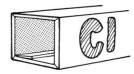

Three folds make a triangular form.

A variety of other free-standing display labels can be made. Scored and folded card of a reasonable thickness will stand on its own accord. With a single fold the label can be displayed as in either A or B below.

To attract particular attention to an item on display it is a good idea to raise the label up from the surface on which the item is resting.

A simple one-fold label can be displayed in two ways.

Label holders

Make saw cuts in little odds and ends of wood. Sand the wood down and insert sturdy card labels into the saw cuts. Make sure the labels stand vertically so they can be clearly seen. An alternative is to cut a slot, using a fine hack saw, into the plastic tops of aerosol cans and insert the labels. The holders can be weighted with a lump of modelling clay if need be.

You can use plastic spine binders, of the type used to hang posters or loose papers together, to make free-standing label holders. Cut the binders into short lengths of about 5 cm to 10 cm, and stick them onto stout, coloured mounting card with strong impact adhesive. Display labels can then be slid into place and changed very quickly as required.

Make saw cuts in odds and ends of wood and insert card labels in the cuts.

Cut a slot for a label in the plastic top of an aerosol can and weight it with modelling clay.

Sections of plastic spine binders make good label holders.

Stick them to card with strong impact adhesive.

For large-scale or particularly long headings designed to extend along the length of a display board, it is a useful idea to glue a length of plastic cupboard tracking along the top of the display board. (Use impact adhesive.) You can then prepare headings and labels on stout card and position them in the tracking above the display.

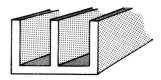

Cross section of door tracking — you'll find it in white, brown and black plastic at most DIY shops.

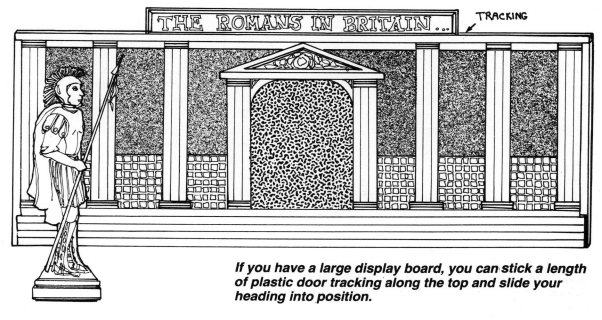

If you have a large display board, you can stick a length of plastic door tracking along the top and slide your heading into position.

Labels as a feature

It is appropriate for labels and headings to become a feature of certain displays. Pictorial headings can be made by writing them within a shape depicting whatever the word means. (See illustrations.)

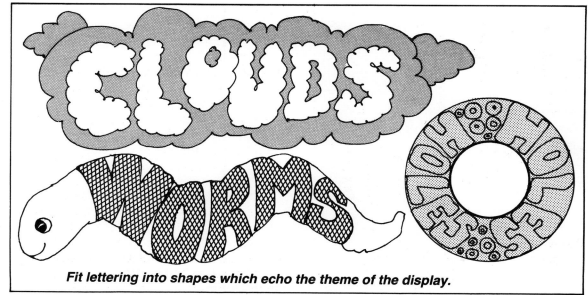

Fit lettering into shapes which echo the theme of the display.

Sometimes it is more effective not to attach labels and headings to the display but to hang them, as mobiles, in front of it. Words can be written on both sides of mobile labels so doubling the amount of information conveyed. The movement of the words attracts attention and consequently the 'message' of the display is reinforced.

Hang words as mobiles in front of a display. You can write on both sides of the labels.

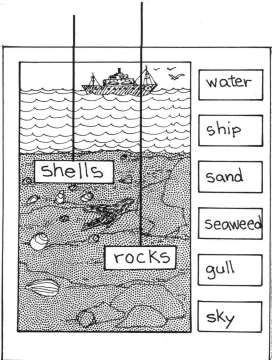

With young children it is often very successful to introduce an element of mystery and fun into headings and labels used in a display. This can be done in a number of ways. If the labels are written on scored and folded pieced of card, they can be displayed with the 'flap' down. The children then lift the flap to find the word hidden beneath it. Alternatively, make cardboard pockets for words on the display. You can empty the pockets and give the labels to the children to put back in the correct pockets.

Lift-the-flap labels are fun.

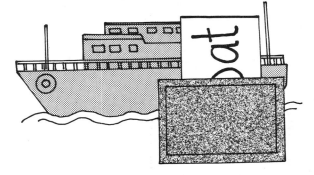

Add 'pockets' to a display and give the children a batch of labels to sort into the right pockets.

A similar way of using labels as a learning aid is to write all the words associated with a display on luggage type labels which the children can hang on large mapping pins strategically placed on the display board. This combines good display with reading and word/picture matching skills.

Put mapping pins on the display so the children can hang luggage type labels in the right place.

Involving the viewer

Captions and headings are very important because they draw children into the display and they should be worded to involve the viewer as much as possible: 'Sara Green is the expert on clocks in class 3; ask her if you want to know more. 'How old do you think this tool is? (Lift the flap for the answer after you have guessed.)' 'What do you think this is for? The photograph on the right shows it in use.' 'This chart shows the pets that people in our class have. Is your pet shown?' 'Watch this space for an unusual object!' 'Look at these drawings of buildings. Can you name them and say where you would find them? Put your answers in the box provided.'

Preparing written work for display

It is a mistake to think that work is only on display if it is put on the wall for all to see. Display also involves the presentation of individual pieces of work in exercise books and folders. In a busy teacher's life, it is all too easy to neglect this aspect of display, but it is surely unreasonable to expect children to continue to think and write imaginatively and creatively if they are always provided with pieces of blank paper of the same shape and size. There are simple ways of encouraging children to improve the quality of their written work by concentrating on the quality of presentation and they will gain satisfaction from this just as much as from having their work exposed.

Decoration and paper

Children learn from seeing examples of good practice; they invariably try to imitate what they see, thus improving the quality of their own efforts. Good layout and balance in a piece of written work are as important as a well-formed style of handwriting.

Borders and illumination
The addition of a carefully designed border, executed with pen and ink or coloured pencils, enhances the appearance of a piece of written work and increases its appeal for the reader. Show children examples of traditional border patterns in books to encourage

Arrange written work in appropriate cut-out shapes. The background can be coloured and decorated.

Careful work on illuminated letters can produce some beautiful results.

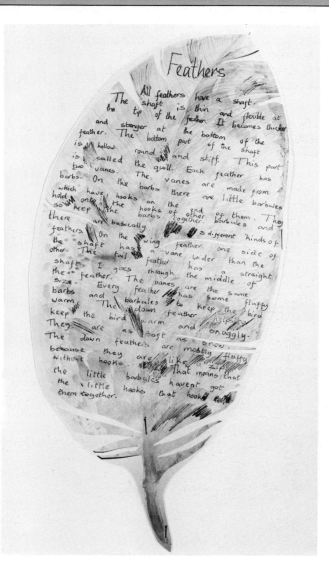

Some of the seeds are different colours that is becaues some of them have dried up and when thing dry up they change colour. Attached to the seed is the stem The stem has hair attached to it at the top They are arranged like the bristles on an old fashioned chimney sweep brush The little white hairs help the seed to float The white hair are spread out Just like the cover of a parachute At first the seed are all together but when the wind blows they all blow away It is good that the blow away becaues is they didnot when all the seed drop off they would drop in the same place and they would not beble to grow

A class of eight-to-ten year olds wrote about seeds and then decorated their work with carefully-detailed drawings. They used stencil patterns to make colourful initial letters. The work was double-mounted on black then white paper to complete a striking display.

them to do the same, in their own way, with their own work.

Most children are fascinated by the illuminated letters used in early manuscripts. If they are asked to begin a piece of written work with a colourful and intricate illuminated letter, they will usually complete the work with particular interest and attention, and the results can be stunning.

Matching paper to theme

Younger children like writing on paper which has been cut out to represent shapes associated with the subject of their writing. This encourages them to use language imaginatively and, of course, makes it easy to use the work for exciting display. Children writing about the Great Fire of London in one class were given pieces of paper which had been scorched brown in a lightly heated oven. The difference which this simple idea made to the quality of their work was most surprising. The effect was further appreciated when the written work was displayed alongside paintings and collages of scenes from the Great Fire.

Marbling

The traditional craft of marbling provides beautiful backgrounds for writing on certain themes and topics. The swirling, colourful patterns lend themselves well to subjects associated with mystery and magic, such as witches and Hallowe'en, caves and underwater caverns.

Marbling is not difficult to do. All you need is a large shallow tray suitable for holding water. Oil-based marbling inks are dropped in random blobs onto the surface of the water and then 'swirled' together using a marbling comb. This is a wide-toothed comb which can be made by driving equally spaced oval nails through a batten of wood. The nails should be between 5 mm and 10 mm apart. By pulling the comb through the tray of water, the oil-based inks will be drawn into exciting and colourful swirling patterns. If a cartridge or a similar weight paper is then dropped onto the surface of the water, the pattern made by the oil-based inks will be transferred onto the paper. Tap the surface of the paper whilst it is floating on the water, to release any air bubbles trapped under the paper. If this is not done, unattractive white blotches will appear in the surface of the patterned paper.

After a few seconds the paper can be lifted from the surface of the water, allowed to drain and laid out to dry. As the surface of the water is constantly moving, so is the pattern of inks, and therefore each final product will be different.

Try to show children examples of traditional marbling patterns on the fly leaves of old books.

Class books

Children enjoy reading each others' work. Work shut away in exercise books becomes a private treaty between the child and the teacher. If written and pictorial work is displayed in class-books, which are available for all children to read, the scope of the work is extended and the children's enthusiasm for it is likely to be increased. Sometimes children's work can be typed for a class-book and illustrated with pictures from colour magazines. (Keep a box of pictures likely to be useful so that children can look for a suitable picture before or after writing.) Hanging colourful and attractively designed class-books in various parts of a school will also demonstrate the importance attached to integrating different skills and areas of the curriculum.

Children enjoy reading each other's work — display it in a class book.

Good use made of colourful and attractive book covers in a junior school library display.

Putting books on show

A fundamental task in any school is to cultivate children's interest in books. Book display, especially in the early years of schooling, is very important. By displaying books well we can:

1 Promote an interest in reading and the enjoyment of literature.
2 Draw attention to new acquisitions.
3 Focus attention and interest upon a book collection dealing with a particular theme or subject area.
4 Use books as a support to other display materials in stimulus and interest displays.
5 Use book illustrations as a means of leading children towards an appreciation of books.

Arranging book areas

Whether schools have a purpose-built library area or simply book corners within classrooms or other parts of the school, consideration should be given to the arrangement and content of such areas.

Good lighting is, of course, essential. If sufficient natural light is not available in the book corner then artificial lighting must be employed. Many of the larger DIY stores sell very effective, yet comparatively cheap, clip-on spot lights. If you have suitable convenient power points, these can be attached to the frames of display boards, the edges of shelves or even to painted broom handles

A carpet to lie on and plenty of light — two essentials in a reading area.

mounted in large flower pots and acting as lamp standards. The spot lights can be angled to shine on the reading area or the book display.

Display units, of the kind described on page 48, can be used to create bays or corners to separate certain parts of a classroom or teaching area from the rest. In a reading corner a table and chairs should be provided but even more essential is a carpet as many children prefer to sit or lie on the floor when absorbed in a book. Large bean bags or scatter cushions make useful additions.

Pictures and attractive posters advertising books will add to the general atmosphere of any book area making it a place where children want to be.

Cover-on displays

Clearly books which are displayed 'cover on' are more likely to capture attention than those which are displayed 'spine on'. Book covers today are, on the whole, extremely attractive and it is worth making the most of this to promote an interest in books and reading.

Books can be displayed 'cover on' with a minimum of expense or effort. They can simply be half opened and stood up on strategic surfaces such as window sills, low cupboard tops or tables where they can be seen and handled by the children. This immediately creates an environment in which books are seen to be important, especially if they are changed regularly. However, this basic method of display is only suitable for hard-backed books and, even then, it imposes a certain degree of

A basic shelf on L-brackets — a retaining strip holds books in place.

If you've got the space, a staggered shelf arrangement looks best.

strain on the spine of the book which may result in damage over a period of time.

Shelving

Books are better displayed on shelving, either commercially produced or improvised. You can screw L-shaped brackets to the wall and make shelves from veneer-coated or laminated board. More elaborate and expensive commercial shelving systems using

ladder strips and brackets provide a more flexible system. If books are to be displayed 'cover on' on shelves of this kind, you should glue or tack a narrow retaining strip along the front edge of the shelf to prevent the books from slipping off. If the shelf is wide enough, you can fix another retaining strip along the middle of the shelf so that it takes a double layer of books.

When space allows, it looks better to

arrange shelves in a staggered formation instead of stacking them one above the other.

When displaying books on open shelves, try to incorporate other display material such as potted plants or pictures and real objects associated with the book theme. Such additions can help to promote an interest which books alone may fail to achieve.

Space for book display in corridor areas is very limited. Shelving units designed for such areas have to be narrow and at the same time accommodate as many books as will fit, displayed as attractively as possible.

Simple display units can be made quickly and comparatively cheaply by constructing a softwood frame into which narrow shelves can be fixed by screwing through the side panels of the outer frame. Arrange the shelves so they can accommodate a variety of sizes of books. Retainer strips, as described earlier, can be fitted to the front edge of the shelves or plastic-covered curtain wires can be stretched between the side panels of the outer frame to serve the same purpose. The whole unit can be painted or varnished and attached to the wall using flat glass or mirror plates screwed to the rear of the top and bottom of the outer frame.

Introducing book display units of this kind into corridor areas, which are often austere and unwelcoming, can make a dramatic transformation not only in the appearance of a school but in children's response to books.

A book display unit made from a softwood frame with narrow shelves screwed to the side panels. Retaining strips make it easy to display books 'cover-on'.

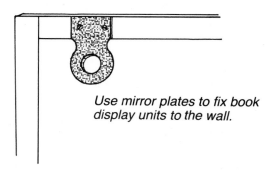

Use mirror plates to fix book display units to the wall.

Displaying open books

Although it is usually best to display books 'cover on', some need to be displayed open at a particular page. Putting open books flat on a horizontal surface is not always appropriate. Simple book rests raise books up from the surface and support them in an open position. You can buy book rests from educational suppliers in various forms, some made from bent chromed wire, others from wood. However, you can also make simple rests from offcuts of plywood and other oddments of wood which can be glued or tacked together, or from stout card which can be scored, folded and stuck together to form sloping supports. The finished book rests can then be painted or covered with self-adhesive vinyl covering.

Book rest in bent chromed wire.

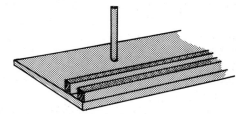

A simple book rest — the open book fits into the slot and leans against the dowel rod.

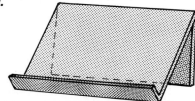

Make book rests from strong card or wood offcuts and paint them or cover them with sticky-back plastic.

A very simple book rest, suitable for hard-backed books, can be made by sticking two parallel pieces of moulding, with a space between them, onto a plywood base and mounting a pillar, made from a dowel rod, towards the back of the base. The bottom edge of the open book rests between the moulding strips, and the back of the book leans against the dowel pillar.

As with any display it is a mistake to overcrowd book displays. Too many books tend to confuse the viewer and diminish the impact of the display.

Cut stout cardboard boxes this way to make book display boxes. Cover with wallpaper or plastic and store books 'cover-on' or 'spine-on'.

'Spine-on' displays

If space does not allow you to display books 'cover on' they can be put 'spine on'. Strong cardboard boxes which have been cut down and covered with plastic in colourful designs make very practical storage boxes in which books can be arranged on either a theme or subject basis. Similar systems can be purchased commercially and are usually supplied as flat packs ready to be made up. A set of such storage boxes will accommodate a large number of books and make for very easy identification if clearly labelled.

A development of the same idea is to make a series of open-fronted boxes from light plywood which can be joined together to make a random 'pigeon hole' effect. The boxes can be painted or covered with adhesive-backed plastic. Carpet tiles can be added to all horizontal surfaces to make the finished product usable as either storage or display units.

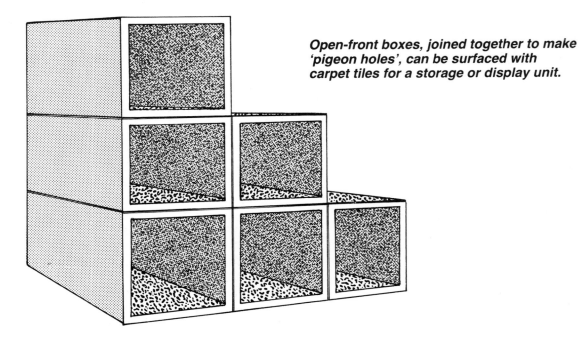

Open-front boxes, joined together to make 'pigeon holes', can be surfaced with carpet tiles for a storage or display unit.

Making the most of the interest table

Most primary classrooms have a nature or interest table. Display on this can range from a haphazard and dusty jumble of natural and man-made objects to a carefully selected arrangement of objects displayed to illustrate a theme or topic. Firstly, attention should be given to the location of the table within the classroom. It is best to put it in a place where it can be backed by a display board to accommodate a variety of support material (children's work, posters, pictures, charts and photographs).

Whatever the size of the surface on which the display is to be made, a variety of levels will add immediate interest to the display (see page 16).

It is usually most effective to group items of a similar kind within a display. For example, in a display showing a seashore collection you could group shells, pebbles, driftwood, starfish and seaweed separately.

Where the aim of a display is predominantly instructive, it is important to name objects clearly and to support them with explicit photographs, descriptive charts and colourful illustrations.

Borrowing

For thematic displays the children can often bring in interesting items. If it is an unusual subject or you have younger children, it may help to send a note home explaining what the display is about. (Do keep a careful note of where everything came from.) Things like stuffed birds and animals, skeletons, costumes etc. not only provide stimulating starting points for classroom work but also extend the scope of displays. Many Local Education Authorities operate their own museum loan services and will provide a supply of exhibits throughout the year to their teachers.

Museums are not the only source of loans. Local businesses, craftsmen and companies are often prepared to help with materials for interest displays. A search through the 'Yellow Pages' may inspire you.

Contact with a blacksmith may secure the loan of an anvil, bellows, tools, horseshoes and other examples of his craft and trade.

Similarly, an approach made to a boat chandler could result in a display of ropes, pulleys, sailcloth, navigational instruments and a host of other interesting exhibits.

If you are fortunate enough to have a local weaver nearby or a County Branch of the Spinners and Weavers Guild, they are often willing to lend a spinning wheel, carding tools, examples of fleeces, spun wool, spindles and shuttles, examples of natural dyes made from berries and mosses and many more fascinating items which will form an interesting stimulus display.

Live exhibits

On nature tables it is often necessary to display live exhibits. However, this is not always done to advantage. Frequently the exhibits are displayed in containers which make viewing difficult because the container is sited at the wrong height or because the lighting is poor. Most water specimens resulting from pond dipping or rock pool searches are best viewed in large, open, shallow trays. These enable bigger groups of children to observe the contents of the tray at the same time. It is even more effective and educationally valuable if live specimens can be viewed under large stand magnifiers or hand magnifiers which can be left on the table for children to use. There is an almost universal excitement amongst children when given the opportunity to view silkworms, earthworms, tadpoles, snails and other 'minibeasts' through a magnifier of some kind.

Due care must, of course, be taken to ensure that live specimens are displayed in containers and positions appropriate for their needs and that they are only displayed for a short time before being returned to their natural habitats. Preparation for such a display should ideally include involvement by the children in considering such questions as: Is there enough depth of water in the container? Is there sufficient room in the container? Are the conditions correct for the creatures under observation?

It is equally important that live specimens should be displayed at a height where children can view them easily and where there is little risk of the exhibits being knocked over or disturbed in any way.

Exhibits such as leaves and grasses often pose problems as to how they can be best displayed. A useful method is to slide them into plastic wallets such as those sold for the storage of overhead projector transparencies. These wallets allow clear observation but at the same time prevent lightweight objects like leaves and feathers from being blown off the display surface.

An alternative is actually to mount the specimens by carefully arranging them on a neutral card background (grey, buff, cream) and then covering them with self-adhesive transparent film which will hold them in place. If this method is used, it is essential to lay the plastic film down onto the items for display, taking care to remove any air bubbles by gently rubbing around the specimens with fingertips.

Items such as flowers, dried grasses and large feathers are best displayed in ceramic vases or stoneware jars.

Colour displays

Colour displays are a feature of many primary classrooms. Collections of items of a single colour are displayed, usually started by the teacher and added to by the children. Fabric shops sometimes help by providing samples of fabric in various shades and tones of a requested colour. Paint shade cards and paper samples will add to the breadth of a colour display.

Colour displays can be extended beyond the simple 'colour table'. In one school where I worked, a 'colour week' was held on occasions during the school year. By far the most impressive was a 'black and white' week. The overall effect of art and craft work, written work and all display being restricted to the stark contrasts of black and white made a considerable impact within the school.

Written work was written and displayed as if to represent newsprint; all display board headings appeared as newspaper headlines. The jumbo typewriter was used to produce some of the written work. All drawings were created by using soft-grade pencils, pen and indian ink and black felt-tipped pens. Cut paper counterchange work and mobiles, based on regular shapes, were made and decorated in black and white.

A similar approach could be adopted with any colour, where tonal qualities could be exploited. Colour displays are designed to make children more aware of colour in their world, so helping them understand more about colour and its uses.

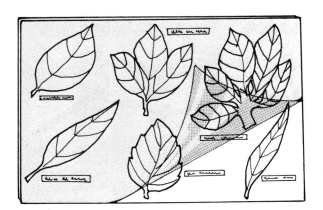

Slide lightweight objects into transparent storage wallets.

Arrange specimens carefully before covering them with self-adhesive transparent film.

Ask children to pick a 'leaf' from a word tree and match it to the right item on a display.

Word trees

A 'word tree' is a useful way of bringing the appropriate vocabulary into a nature display. A branch of a tree of a suitable size and shape is fixed in a flower tub full of sand or soil. Words relating to items displayed on the nature table can be written or printed on leaf shapes cut from thin card. These can then be hung on the branches of the tree. Children can be invited to pick a leaf from the tree and match it to the appropriate item on display. 'Word trees' of this kind can be incorporated into all kinds of displays where trees would be a natural feature, such as the seasons, the countryside, etc.

Sustaining interest

You can add interest and fun to some displays by introducing an element of mystery. An unusual item, unlikely to be known by the children, can be placed on a display box with a large question mark on it or a label asking 'What is it?' Put an 'answer box' underneath for the children's suggestions. These can be read out, discussed and finally voted on before the answer is revealed.

The display on a nature or interest table should be changed regularly if it is to hold children's attention and be seen as something of importance. Sometimes a group of children can be given sole responsibility for setting up a display on a subject of particular interest to them. They will learn a lot about display and their classmates will look particularly carefully at the results!

Entrance and assembly halls

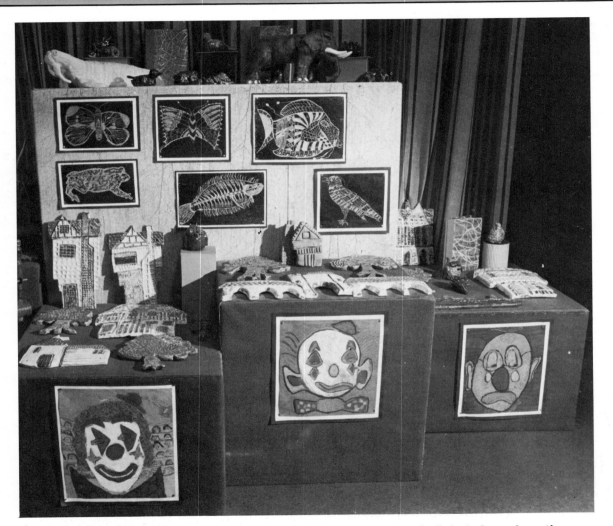

A wide variety of children's work in a primary school entrance hall. Labels and captions are not always necessary in display like this.

Particular attention should be given to the display in an entrance hall as most children in the school will pass through this area during the day. It will also give parents and visitors their first impression of the school.

In many schools classes take it in turns to provide entrance hall displays. As different teachers have different strengths and interests, their approach to display varies accordingly. Therefore, over a period of time, most curriculum areas will be covered.

In the assembly hall

Displays in assembly halls can create considerable problems. Assembly halls in most primary schools have to serve many purposes: they are a place of worship, a gymnasium, a sports hall, a dining hall and a drama studio. Therefore, a variety of activities will be taking place around any display, and this should be taken into account when it is set up.

The amount of space available is often very restricted and it is difficult to find space to accommodate three-dimensional displays where they won't be in the way and where the items on display are safe.

It is also hard to find wall space at a height at which children can see the display properly, but this particular problem can sometimes be solved. As it is mostly large-scale work which is displayed in assembly halls, the children can stand at a distance to view the work on the walls, as if in a gallery, and therefore the height at which it is displayed is not quite so critical. Think of your school hall as a gallery and it may give you new ideas of how it can be used.

If wall space is lacking, you can display on boards suspended from the ceiling or beams. Displaying work on windows is seldom successful. The work tends to fall off rather quickly; fading is a great problem; it is difficult to see the work properly and it looks very unsightly from the outside. The exception is work meant to have light shining through it – like stained-glass-effect pictures.

Using the corners

If it is possible to accommodate three-dimensional displays in the school assembly hall at all, then the extreme corners are usually best. Rolls of coloured corrugated cardboard can be opened out to stand round the two sides of a corner and held in position by the use of double-sided adhesive pads. Display boxes can be arranged in front of this backing.

Remember that displays in the hall may become disarranged more quickly than in other parts of the school and frequent checking and changing will therefore be needed to keep a display looking attractive. A poorly presented or neglected display serves very little purpose.

The school assembly hall, like the entrance hall, is used by all the children and staff. Any display sited in a school hall will, therefore, be seen and enjoyed by the whole school community. This is a fundamental principle of good display: that it is a shared expression requiring a shared response. In such a vital position, a display can become either a springboard for further work or the culmination and celebration of a term's work for a particular class or year group.

Large-scale projects

School halls also allow the display of work on a larger scale than is possible in a classroom. Children enjoy working on a large co-operative project with life-size illustrations. The problem which arises with working on such a large scale is how to display the finished product. The very size and weight of the work creates its own problems. It makes the task more manageable if the work is planned and produced in sections. These can then be assembled in the display area.

Pulley systems

If you don't have permanent display boards in your hall, a pulley system can

be installed above a suitable expanse of wall. The pulleys can be small and unobtrusive and the ropes are attached to a long rigid batten into which a series of hooks have been screwed. Large sheets of pinboard or similar material (usually 8 ft. by 4 ft.) with holes drilled along the top edge to correspond with the hooks in the batten can be used when large displays are wanted. The advantages of the 'pulley system' are:

1 The pinboard sheets are easy to store and manoeuvre.
2 Work for display can be prepared and then mounted on the board when it is flat on the hall floor. This eliminates the problems of trying to hold work in a vertical position while it is being fixed to the board and means that steps and ladders aren't needed.
3 When they aren't needed for display, the boards attached to the pulley batten can be used as backdrops for dramatic productions.

When the work has been mounted on the display board, the board can be hooked to the batten and then pulled into position.

Display large scale work with the help of a pulley system. Mount the work on a pinboard before hooking it to the batten and pulling it into position.

Building free-standing displays

So far I have dealt chiefly with fixed display boards and arrangements of improvised units for the display of three-dimensional work.

It is not always possible or appropriate to set up displays in the same place. Sometimes you have to put displays in places where there are no display boards and limited wall space. How is it best to do this?

Commercial systems

There are many commercial systems available consisting of separate display boards which interlock, using a variety of fixings, to provide interestingly shaped and large-scale display areas. Most systems use pinboard as the basic material, covered in coloured and textured hessians and felts. Generally speaking these systems look very attractive and present few storage problems as they stack flat. They can also be added to as and when funds allow or the need arises. A school can, therefore, build up a display system over a period of time. Display systems of this kind are, however, expensive and beyond the scope of many schools.

Making your own systems

It is possible for schools to build their own systems much more cheaply. Sheets of pinboard of the required size can be mounted on a wood batten frame. The surface of the board can be covered with hessian or felt using a Trigger Tacker gun or left uncovered until it is used. Finally L-section plastic angle can be fixed around the edges of the board to serve as a border and to protect the edges of the pinboard from damage. Boards made in this way and then fitted with pillar hinges can be freely connected and disconnected to make a variety of arrangements possible.

These display boards can be arranged down the centre of a school hall in a zig-zag fashion or put around the edge of a hall to form bays. Both sides of the board can be used. Although designed as display boards, a system of this kind can also be used as 'scenery flats' for dramatic productions.

Mount pinboard on a batten frame and attach pillar hinges to make versatile display boards.

Thematic displays

Special occasions

Providing original displays for the major events in the school calendar is always a problem. Each year the thought of finding new ways of presenting the familiar themes of autumn, harvest, Hallowe'en, Guy Fawkes night, Christmas, winter, spring, Easter, summer and other popular topics daunts many teachers. If you can occasionally break right away from the conventional ways of displaying work or exhibits and present them in a completely different and often unexpected way, it is well worth the extra time and effort involved.

Hallowe'en

For Hallowe'en a corner of the classroom can be converted to a witches' cavern by hanging and draping black fabric and crêpe paper from the ceiling or beams and covering existing furniture with suitable coloured drapes so as to create an atmosphere of mystery and eeriness. Finish off with artwork of bats, spiders and black cats hung as mobiles and large masks of witches' faces painted in fluorescent paint, positioned around the whole display area. Sitting amongst all this, children will find it easier to think and write about witches and spells, potions and travels.

The witches' cavern is just the place to read the class book of spells.

Guy Fawkes

The centrepiece for a Guy Fawkes display in the corner of our school hall consisted of a 'mock' bonfire built from tree branches and cardboard tubes, with a magnificent guy crowning the top of the pile. Red, yellow and orange tissue paper was screwed up and inserted between the branches to simulate flames. Larger 'flames' were cut from metallic foil paper in red, gold and silver and arranged around the fire.

On display boards behind the bonfire were brilliantly-coloured wax resist and paper batik pictures of firework displays and bonfire parties.

Christmas

Christmas presents particular problems of its own. Frequently the whole essence of the celebration of Christmas becomes lost amongst a plethora of coloured metallic foil paper and unimaginable quantities of red and white paint. Remember here that the simplest ideas produce the most effective results. It is well to restrict the range of colours you use – you can see how this works in the window displays of large department stores. If you are using coloured metallic foil, for example, you could restrict yourselves to *one* of these colour combinations:

green and silver	red and gold
blue and silver	green and gold
red and silver	silver and gold
green and red	

An agreed theme for decorations also imposes an order which is much more

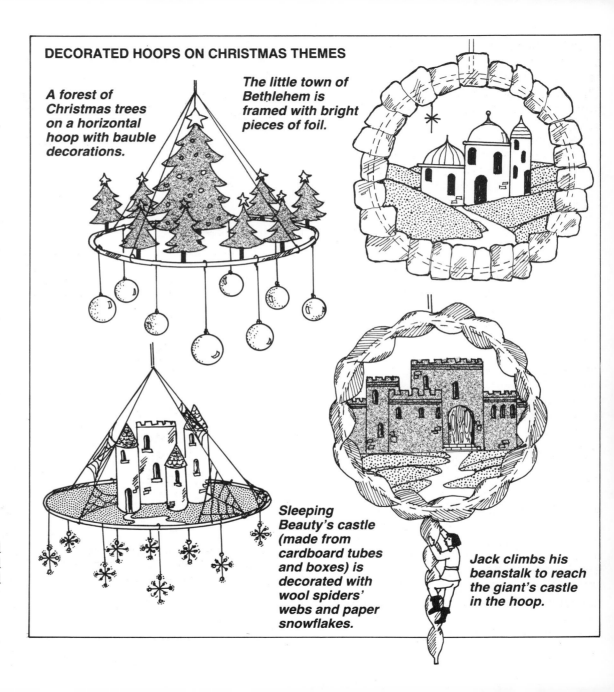

DECORATED HOOPS ON CHRISTMAS THEMES

A forest of Christmas trees on a horizontal hoop with bauble decorations.

The little town of Bethlehem is framed with bright pieces of foil.

Sleeping Beauty's castle (made from cardboard tubes and boxes) is decorated with wool spiders' webs and paper snowflakes.

Jack climbs his beanstalk to reach the giant's castle in the hoop.

effective than a random, haphazard collection of ideas. Themes like pantomime titles, pantomime characters, Christmas carols or Christmas songs provide an opportunity for a variety of interpretations. A series of decorations based upon hoops hung from the ceiling or beams creates a striking display in the school hall. The hoops can be covered around their circumference only or be completely covered by sticking paper all over them. If the whole surface of the hoop is to be covered, it has to be done on both sides. On hoops hung horizontally, decorative images can be arranged on the horizontal surface or hung from the perimeter of the hoop. Use three-dimensional images on horizontal surfaces and two- or three-dimensional ones on vertical surfaces.

To provide relief images, polystyrene cut with a hot wire cutter is a most useful material. The surface of polystyrene can be coloured either with paint or with water-based felt-tipped pen. Use double-sided vinyl tape or adhesive pads to fix the images to the surfaces.

The Christmas Nativity scene requires a considerable amount of thought and planning. Assess the space available to determine what scale your scene should be. Small children are generally most impressed by things on a large scale. One of the simplest ways of creating large figures is by building up newspaper effigies around cut broom handles mounted in rounders' post bases. You can paint and dress the figures to represent whatever characters you need.

BUILDING UP LARGE FIGURES

Mount a cut-down broom handle in a rounders' post base. Bend coat-hanger wire around for arms.

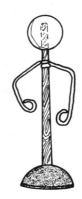

Cover a ball of newspaper with white tissue paper and tape it to the broom handle with vinyl tape.

Tape pads of folded newspaper to the arms and cover with white tissue. Fold sheets of newspaper and tape them to the broom handle at neck level — splay out and attach to the base.

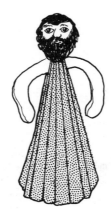

Paint the face and add fur or crepe for beards and hair. Dress by pinning fabric to the paper foundation.

A group of finished nativity figures.

The series of diagrams shows the building up of basic figures, while the photograph shows some finished Nativity figures. The finished figures can be arranged in a suitable setting.

Use a minimum of background to symbolise the stable, spread some straw on display boxes, hang a carefully-made star above, and you will have a display which captures the appropriate atmosphere on a scale large enough to be seen and enjoyed by the whole school.

Help from the community

I have always found that people within a local community are only too pleased to help the neighbourhood school with displays for special occasions. A harvest display in one village school yielded ground flour from a local mill, various examples of seed from a neighbouring farmer, a harvest loaf made in the shape of a sheaf of corn complete with mouse from a local baker, and a real sheaf of wheat from yet another farmer. This, combined with the generosity of the children and their parents added up to a magnificent harvest display which was enjoyed by everyone associated with the school. A combination of children's work plus an arrangement of interesting outside exhibits provides a good balance for a successful display.

It is sometimes possible to arrange a 'split display' where two displays on the same theme in different parts of the school are linked. A boat and oars, borrowed from a local fisherman and

sited outside the main entrance of a school, provided a direct link with a display indoors of borrowed fishing nets, floats, items of fishermen's clothing, hooks and other objects such as shells, driftwood, pebbles and seaweed brought in by the children themselves. The display was completed by the children's imaginative and thought-provoking paintings, drawings, poetry and prose.

When a boat is needed and no such outside help is available, an upturned

table with shaped, cut out and painted sides attached to the legs will make an effective model boat. It could be used as a centre piece for a display on Vikings, Elizabethan explorations, the coast etc.

Local studies display

The photograph below shows part of a local studies display which was sited in the corner of a corridor. The work was done by a mixed class of third and fourth year juniors. A selection of paintings,

The corner of two corridors in a junior department made into an exciting display area for two- and three-dimensional work on a local studies project.

drawings and clay 'slab work' houses combined with factual evidence in the form of charts showing the use of the various buildings in the village street and what they were made from provided the material for the display. This display was linked with another, set up in the children's classroom, showing a completely different approach. It was an informative display, mainly showing the materials which are used in present-day building. These had been lent by parents who were, therefore, keen to accept an invitation to come into school to find out what the children had been learning about and to see how their contribution had helped.

This raises an important point about help given with displays. Whenever possible, people who have helped in any way with the setting up of a display should be invited into school to see the final result. This clearly helps to forge good relationships generally and opens up further possibilities for the future as one contact frequently leads to another.

Feature displays

Display should not be thought of solely in terms of what is attached to display boards or viewed on display units. 'Feature displays' in which children become physically involved, are frequently among the most successful of all displays. However, considerable time and effort is involved in preparing them, so it is important that you are clear in your own mind what the educational aims and

objectives of the exercise are.

The Jack-in-the-box in the photograph below was created from an unwanted tea chest covered with eye-catching shiny vinyl sheeting. The figure was made from a variety of materials including papier mâché for the

head, rubber gloves for the hands and padded clothing, supported on a broom handle, for the body. Younger children in the school were greatly attracted by this display and it served to introduce them to colour recognition, which was the aim of the display.

A large 'Jack in the Box' clown emerging from a converted tea chest in an infant school entrance hall made an eye-catching introduction to colour recognition.

On another occasion, the same tea chest, redecorated with painted wood grain sides could become a pirates' treasure chest or a buried treasure trove.

Some old clothes, stuffed with straw and other scraps, with the addition of a stuffed head made from old tights with added features, produced a very effective 'Worzel Gummidge' as the centre piece for a display of creative writing on the theme of 'Talking Scarecrows'.

Action displays

Infant classrooms often feature 'action displays'. In one infant classroom I saw a splendid castle, constructed from cardboard boxes which had been covered with white paper and painted by using large sponges dipped in paint. This became a 'live' experience for the children. They had built the castle, they could live within its boundaries and they were able, through their rôle play, to live a little closer to history. The venture transformed the room. Naturally, it created some temporary problems as space was restricted for other activities but, for the time the castle existed, the children were very much involved with a real educational experience.

In another school the centre of a first year junior classroom was cleared to make room for a floor-to-ceiling size space ship, constructed from large cardboard cartons covered with silver and gold metallic foil paper. The base carton was equipped with a hinged door (vinyl tape was used to make the hinge) to allow one or two children at a time to

enter the spacecraft.

For the duration of this display, which was the culmination of a term's work on the universe, the children were seated, and consequently spent their working day, around the central feature. This created an atmosphere which resulted in some extremely perceptive work. The central element of the display was supported by paintings, drawings, prints and written work, some of which was mounted in a class-book shaped as a spacecraft.

It is often the simplest ideas which capture the imagination of young children. If children arrive at school and find that cardboard, paint and a lot of imagination have converted their classroom door to a dungeon door, church door or entrance to a space capsule, they respond immediately and their work is consequently enriched.

What happened to our classroom door?

Ideas for simpler displays

Whilst most of the displays described in this chapter reflect the time and effort given by imaginative and enthusiastic teachers to produce stimulating and visually exciting displays, others can be simpler in content and yet still demand attention.

One of the most poignant Easter displays I've seen consisted of a simple wooden cross, about 2 m in height, set in the grass at the top of a school drive. All the children had to pass the cross on their way to the playground.

Tube figures

Features of the school building can be used to create simple displays. For example, many modern schools are of basic girder construction which means that many metal box section pillars are left exposed internally, and these can be used most effectively to accommodate tube figures which can either be stuck, using double-sided vinyl tape, or tied to the pillars.

The basic structure of tube figures remains the same even though, with slight decorative adaptations, the character of the figure may change from choirboy to shepherd or wise man.

Tube figures are made from full flat sheets of card, the size depending upon the scale of the finished figure required. Six-sheet-thickness card is suggested for the head and body section of the figures.

TUBE FIGURES

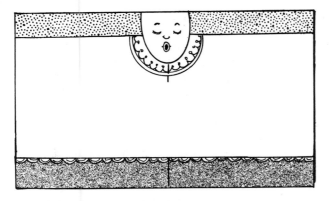

Use six-sheet-thickness card. Mark the flat card with the features etc. of the chosen figure (a choirboy in this example).

Cut the arms from a piece of folded card.

The arms opened out (they hinge at the centre of the book).

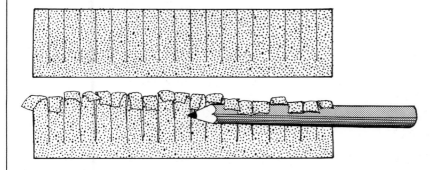

Make cuts in a strip of black sugar paper, and roll it tightly round a pencil to form the hair.

Roll the card into a tube and hold in place with paper fasteners or staples from a long-arm stapler.

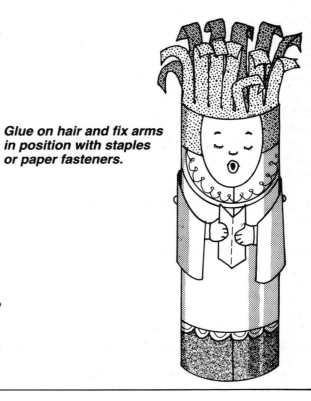

Glue on hair and fix arms in position with staples or paper fasteners.

Outside the school

Obviously, most display is for the benefit of children working inside the school. However, there are many ways in which display can move outside the school walls.

Using the windows

Work displayed on windows need not show only its unattractive back to the world. You can use double-sided window mounts and slide work into them back-to-back so that one piece faces outside. This provides a welcoming link between the school and the outside community.

DOUBLE-SIDED WINDOW MOUNTS

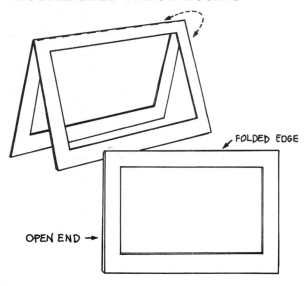

FOLDED EDGE

OPEN END →

The mount can be made by folding a large piece (A2 size) of firm card and cutting a window mount in each side. Fix the edges of the mount on three sides using either a thin trail of PVA adhesive, or a glue stick or pen, or double-sided vinyl tape, and leave one side open so the work can be inserted.

Fired clay work

If you are lucky enough to have a pottery kiln then you can, of course, display fired clay work in selected positions outside the school building.

Both once-fired biscuit ware and glaze-fired ware are suitable for creating decorative displays on external walls, low flat roof areas and in school entrance porches. Slabwork, made from rolled sheet clay, showing a wide variety of images such as fish, birds, local buildings or other landmarks, modes of transport, portraits or figures engaged in a range of school activities, can be fixed to brickwork either by sticking it on with an impact adhesive, or by using masonry nails or plugs and screws.

Display large clay work models which have been constructed by either coiling or slabwork, or perhaps a combination of both, on low flat roof areas or around the grounds on raised platform areas made from decorative wall screening blocks or bricks. Naturally, work displayed in this

way may be vandalised but I have found this occurs surprisingly rarely — possibly because it is children's work that is being displayed. However, the risk should obviously be considered when you are siting displays outside.

Porch areas, leading to main entrances, provide another area for the display of work where it can be seen to advantage and extend a welcome to everyone coming into the school. Thumb pots,

Share the school's work with the world outside.

which have been made leaving a small hole in the bottom, can be decorated, inverted, fitted with a clapper and hung as a wind chime outside all the entrances used by the children.

Display gardens

In some schools it is possible for parts of the school grounds to be designated as 'display gardens'. Here a variety of objects can be displayed to stimulate the children's interest. You might display a collection of old agricultural implements and tools lent by a local farmer, or a display of building materials including different kinds of bricks or decorative chimney pots lent and set up by a local builder. You can approach parents and other local people to see if you can establish a regular series of 'outside displays' if space and other conditions make this possible.

To extend a school's interpretation of display outside the buildings in this way is to add a new dimension to the whole purpose and function of display in schools. From the time the children arrive in the school grounds they are greeted by their own work, displayed for everyone to share. This is also an appropriate way of showing outsiders what the school's attitude is towards visual communication.

Children's clay work in the entrance porch provides a pleasing introduction to a primary school. The wind chimes are made from thumb pots.

Children of all ages modelled their own faces in clay for this floor-to-ceiling panel.

Where to get materials

TOOLS

Staple gun (Trigger Tacker)
E. J. Arnold & Son Ltd., Butterley Street, Leeds 10 (and most other educational suppliers).

Ram or push pin tool
Thomas & Easter, 23a George Street, Baker Street, London W1.

Turikan hook stapler
Panda Binding Systems, 426 Wakefield Road, Denby Dale, Huddersfield, HD8 8QD.

Eyelet hole punch
Dryad Ltd., Northgates, Leicester. Nottingham Handicraft Ltd., 17 Ludlow Hill Road, Melton Road, West Bridgeford, Nottingham.

Most educational suppliers carry a range of scissors, craft knives, staplers and general tools.

Rotary trimmer
Hestair Hope Ltd., 51 Philips Drive, Royton, Oldham.
E.J. Arnold (address above).

DISPLAY SYSTEMS/SCREENS

Midscreen, Econoscreen, Big screen
Marler Haley (Barnet) Ltd., 76 High Street, Barnet, Herts.
Buckley Displays Ltd., 5 Clevemede House, Reading, Berks.

BACKING MATERIALS

Rolls of coloured corrugated card
Spicer Conran Ltd., Cavendish Road, Stevenage, Herts.

Hessian, felt and other fabrics suitable for drapes and backgrounds
Dryad or Nottingham Handicraft (address above).

Bargain bundles of hessian and felt
Warringer Warehouses, Station Road, King's Langley, Herts.

The rotary trimmer—safe for children.

ADHESIVES

Double sided adhesive pads
Cranthorpe Milner & Co. Ltd., 483 Hale End Road, London E4 9PT.

Blu tack, Pritt Buddies, glue pens, glue sticks
Available from most educational suppliers.

HAND AND STAND MAGNIFIERS

Minispector, L.E.M., Midispector, Magnispector
COIL, Combined Optical Industries Ltd., 200 Bath Road, Slough, Bucks.
Osmiroid Educational, E. S. Perry Ltd., Osmiroid Works, Gosport, Hants.

SHALLOW TRAYS/STORAGE CONTAINERS

G. P. G. Containers, G. P. G. International Ltd., Luton Road, Dunstable, Beds.

Mapping pens
Available from most stationers.

Most of the materials for display work suggested in this book are not of a specialist nature and are available from most educational suppliers, DIY stores or stationers.

Notices and labels to copy

On the following pages you will find a selection of notices and labels that are designed to be photocopied. You can use them to provide a co-ordinated labelling style around the school — in classrooms, corridors, staffroom and library. Some are complete notices which can be pasted on card and used as they are. Others are for chopping up to stick on bookshelves, containers, cupboards, notice-boards etc.

Welcome to our school

S'sh! We're reading!

Visitors – please go to the office

Our work on

What's for dinner today?

Whose job is it?

Please wipe your shoes

rubbers   rulers   scissors   pencils
scrap paper   paint   clay   plasticine
printing ink   glue   brushes   string
fabric   paint   brushes   paper clips
drawing ink   chalk   crayons
paper fasteners   printing rollers
glue spreaders   charcoal   pens
elastic bands   drawing pins

Today is: Monday Tuesday Thursday Wednesday Friday January February March April May

June September

July October

August November

December Today's

birthdays clubs

1 2 3 4 5 6 7

8 9 10 11 12 13

14 15 16 17 18 19

20 21 22 23 24 25

26 27 28 29 30 31

Weather: sunny cool warm snowy hot windy frosty rainy stormy cold cloudy showery

Nature table

Interest table

Book corner

Reading   Maths

Library – quiet please

Please walk – don't run!

Fiction Story books
Information books Plays
Non-fiction Dictionaries
Reference Poetry books
Anthologies Song books
Bibles and hymn books
Encyclopaedias

Animals Birds
Flowers Insects
Mini-beasts Pets
Plants Pond life
Trees Zoos

Health Our bodies
Ourselves Senses

Bicycles
Cars Flight
Railways Roads
Ships Space
Transport
Canals

Bridges Building
Castles Churches
Clothes Costume
Farming Fishing
Food
Homes and Houses
Cookery

Dinosaurs Egyptians Greeks
How we used to live Middle Ages
Prehistoric man Normans Romans
Twentieth century Tudors & Stuarts
Victorians Vikings

Coal Deserts Earth
Electricity Energy
Minerals Mountains
Oil Polar regions
Rivers
Rocks and fossils
Sea Volcanoes
Weather Water

Communications

Government

Local studies

Our environment

People who help us

Jobs

American Indians

Cowboys

Eskimos   Gypsies

Pirates and smugglers

Wars & soldiers

Astronomy

Computers

Engineering

Entertainment

Exploration

Festivals

Hobbies

Jokes and riddles

Photography

Religions   Science

Signs & symbols

Sport

Australia

Canada

Eire

England

New Zealand

Scotland

Wales

Ulster

Other countries

Software Audio-visual aids

Slides Records Tapes

Posters Wall charts Films

Film strips Videos Broadcasts

Radiovision Catalogues

OHP transparencies

Record cards Registers

Caretaker Cleaners
Head teacher
Staff toilet
Boys' Girls' toilets
Please close the door

Staffroom

Enquiries Library

Lost property

Fire alarm Office

First aid Secretary

Staff meeting

Maths Drama Art and craft
Language development RE
Science Health education
Movement Music History
Management Geography
Social studies PE Reading
Tea money Dinner duty
Timetable Playground duty

Please switch off the light

Have you washed your hands?

Please knock

When you've used it –
please put it back!

Have you turned the tap off?

Please come back later

Question Answer

Post box   Cricket

Netball   Recorder

Football   Guitar

Photography Chess